DeMystifying the Virtual Desktop

Starting with Desktop Virtualization

Michael Fox

© 2010 by Michael Fox

Cover design by Michael Fox

Interior graphics by Michael Fox

All rights reserved.

No part of this book may be reproduced in any form or by any electronic or mechanical means including information storage and retrieval systems, without permission in writing from the author. The only exception is by a reviewer, who may quote short excerpts in a review.

Limit of Liability and Disclaimer of Warranty: The author has used his best efforts in preparing this book, and the information provided herein is provided "as is." The author makes no representation or warranties with respect to the accuracy or completeness of the contents of this book and specifically disclaims any implied warranties of merchantability or fitness for any particular purpose and shall in no event be liable for any loss of profit or any other commercial damage, including but not limited to special, incidental, consequential, or other damages.

Trademarks: This book identifies product names and services known to be trademarks, registered trademarks, or service marks of their respective holders. They are used throughout this book in an editorial fashion only. Use of a term in this book should not be regarded as affecting the validity of any trademark, registered trademark, or service mark.

Michael Fox
Visit book website at www.demystifyingthevirtualdesktop.com

Printed in the United States of America

First Printing: October 2010

ISBN - 978-1-45630-469-0

To my wife Melanie. Thank you.

Thank You

There are many people I want to thank for their help with this book. To the peer reviewers, thank you very much for your contributions and support. You have all made this a much better book.

To Michelle and Melanie, my editors, thank you for putting me through what has seemed like an endless amount of writing and rewriting. This is a readable book because of you.

To Bill Ayers from the San Francisco Writers Community, your advice and unique perspective has been invaluable.

Thanks to each and every one of you, as well as my supportive friends and family, for your contributions, thoughts and advice.

In alphabetical order:

- Bill Ayers from The San Francisco Writers Community
  Advisor
- Guise Bule from TuCloud
  Peer Reviewer
- Michelle Burns from The Word Zone
  Editor
- Melanie Fox
  Editor
- Tim Grosshuesch from IVDesk
  Peer Reviewer
- Kashif Khwaja from EMC
  Peer Reviewer
- Aaron Kizer from Dell
  Peer Reviewer
- Natalie Lambert from Citrix
  Peer Reviewer
- Dave Payne from Payne, Inc.
  Advisor
- Dave Stark from EMC
  Peer Reviewer

Contents

Introduction: Changing the Game   7

1: Users are people. Users are employees. Sometimes users are just users.   11

2: The Six-Legged Stool   27

3: Desktop Assessments   45

4: Design Analysis for Virtual Desktop Solutions   61

5: Let's Talk Virtual Desktops   95

Conclusion: Let the Games Begin   107

Introduction: Changing the Game

Blatant technical change is something to which many of us have become accustomed. Every year there are newer phones, faster PCs, smaller portable electronics, new ways to obtain information, and higher speeds of Internet access. Technical innovations are featured on the same news programs reporting on world events, leaving us "waiting" for the next technology breakthrough. In fact, some have become such an important part of our daily lives we ask ourselves, "How did I make it through the day before I had this?"

What about the trends that aren't as blatant, but no less powerful and game-changing? Desktop virtualization is a technology shift that is happening *right now* and will soon completely change how we use our computers to do our jobs. So, what does desktop virtualization really mean? Chances are, if you have picked up this book, you already suspect something big is happening. Maybe someone has approached you about the idea, or maybe you are on the tip of taking the plunge into this technology. Or, it could be that you are already experimenting.

Desktop virtualization is not a blatant technology. It may never be. It is a game-changing technology.

Opposite desktop virtualization, the surge in the use of server virtualization has occurred because organizations have discovered it is an idea that makes sense. You take some software, a hypervisor, and install it onto a physical server. You then have the ability to take a large number of physical servers and run them on top of the hypervisor software. The result is that you have now decoupled the operating system from the hardware that it runs on. The resulting virtual machines are now easy to move, back up and manage.

With the ability to put thousands of machines under the umbrella of one virtualization management system, organizations save on server costs, management costs, and operating costs. These are very clear value propositions that are easy to understand.

During the time server virtualization was being adopted, the technologies that make up the virtual desktop were maturing. Some designs existed for the virtual desktop, but they were crude and not understood outside of small technical communities. Some of the component technologies were very mature or, in technical terms, *old*. They were being used to service millions of users around the globe. Others still needed work. Some still do.

That was the past. Sometime, somewhere, the virtual desktop became very real. It wasn't just one thing that made this possible, more the fact that the ingredients became refined enough to put them together to solve problems. If a solution is well implemented, it can completely transform the PC experience. You can make it faster and easier to manage. You can put it in places that are more secure and send it places it couldn't go before. You can make it operate like a utility, and you can make it *reliable*.

However, if you do a poor job of implementation, your creation will fall apart and cause employees enormous levels of frustration, not to mention placing a big red mark on company revenue and productivity. While improving user experience and productivity are by far one of the most important aspects to desktop virtualization, they may not be the drivers for your particular project.

A single virtual desktop is not hard to understand, but the complexity of hundreds or thousands in one system can sometimes be overwhelming. There are numerous moving parts, each with business and technical interdependencies, and dozens of technology combinations, different design choices, and the potential to impact all sorts of established business and technical procedures.

Innovation in this area is rapid and brings with it large quantities of educational marketing material. This material is written to illicit a response from the audience — but instead leaves most people new to the ideas and concepts with half of the story, or often times with more questions than answers.

This book will not answer all of your virtual desktop questions, but it will...

- give you a solid foundation to start building your understanding of the virtual desktop world,
- help you look at the people that will experience this technology in the right way,
- outline how you should start working with and making decisions about these technologies,
- expose you to some of the exciting changes virtual desktops could bring to your company, and
- explain the "big picture" view of the technical concepts you need to know in an easy-to-understand, non-technical, and straightforward way.

On a personal note, when I began writing this book, the goal was simple. I wanted it to be available to the people I speak with every day about this technology as a resource for any technical skill level. I wanted this book to empower them with general knowledge about virtual desktops, and practical advice about how to start working with the different components. My hope was that readers would save some money and find more success because their projects were better planned and more carefully executed.

I felt it was important to do all of this in a completely agnostic way that was not linked to any specific vendor. By doing it in this way, I also wanted to empower my peers around the globe, no matter what technologies they sell or implement, with a resource they could use to help decision makers understand how to begin their virtual desktop journey.

Every day hundreds of millions of people use desktop PCs to do their work. The PC is a fundamental piece of modern technology. It is one of, if not the, most critical tool of the modern age. Now there are people like me out there working to change it. To better it. To *virtualize* it.

Let's get started — we have hundreds of millions of desktops to transform.

Chapter 1:
Users are people. Users are also employees. Sometimes users are just users.

The most important customers of a virtual desktop project are the people that will be using the technology to do their work. Before you begin a discussion or make any decisions at all about virtual desktops, it is important you understand that users are sometimes people, sometimes employees, and often times just users. If you haven't already, from this point forward you must place your users on a pedestal and make all of your decisions with them staring down at you asking the question:

"Will this solution work for me?"

Virtual desktop technologies can dramatically enhance the user experience, or they can be nearly seamless replacements users barely recognize as a change. They are certainly game-changing tools for the users, employees and people you work with.

The many different components of virtual desktops will be defined later in this book. If you are completely new to the idea of virtualization, all you need to understand at this point is that virtualization is a term for a type of technology that inserts a layer of abstraction between technical elements. Most often this is spoken of in terms of server virtualization and the idea that server operating systems are run on top of other pieces of software called hypervisors. These resulting servers are called *virtual machines* since for all intents and purposes they pretty much operate exactly like regular physical servers.

Unlike the server counterpart, desktop virtualization involves not only abstracting the operating system from the hardware, but also applications from the operating system and user configurations from the applications. It often means the removal of the physical PC from the end user. A virtual desktop is made up of a number of different parts, or layers, that operate together to create the user's desktop. The result is that it may operate more quickly or with fewer errors. The data that resides on it might be stored centrally so that it is more secure. Users might be able to access their applications in more than one way, from more than one kind of device. While it looks and acts just like a physical desktop, a virtual desktop represents several abstracted layers working together to present themselves to the end user.

So what about users, people and employees? Why is the first chapter of a book on desktop virtualization about users, people and employees? Quite simply it is because the people using virtual desktops are the ones that determine if the technology is applied in an effective and usable way. If the users have a poor experience, the solution is not operating well and it is reducing their satisfaction and their productivity.

Fair warning—the following views of users, employees and people might take you to a place you haven't explored before. In fact, it might be uncomfortable for some who do not typically hold the user in high regard, or consider what is best for the user as a real person or as an employee.

People are Different

Let's start with your first lesson regarding virtual desktop technology. You, and by extension, your company's virtual desktop technologies, deal with people, not with users or employees. Every single one of us is different, special and unique. Let's stick with the first word in the list —*different*—and discuss why this characteristic is so important and relevant to virtual desktops.

Every person in your company has technology needs that differ slightly from everyone else's. Don't believe it? Does everyone have the same monitor position, keyboard or computer layout? Screen resolution? Location? Hours? Applications? The answer to this question is obviously no. Absolutely no one has the exact same technology needs as the next person. This is a simple truth, but it can have some profound consequences in how you think about people and the application of technology in your company.

To deal with the problem of individual user needs, common practice is to abstract people and all of their differences into groups. Many times these groups are aligned around a particular function or role. Sometimes there are lots of groups with subgroups and further customizations. Other times there will be very few groups with little to no distinction. Once individuals have been put into groups and their settings are managed, it can be said with confidence, and sometimes with arrogance, that we are meeting people's technology needs.

This kind of abstraction can be seen when you consider the needs of different groups. For example, a call center might have desktops with two monitors that access a number of applications. A sales group might have laptops using remote-access software to allow them to work from anywhere. Even with these groupings and moderate levels of customization, most people in most organizations are given a set of tools that are relatively the same.

Within these top-level groups, organizations separately address (or maybe not) the needs of each subgroup, and sometimes each individual. This is typically done by adding or removing certain applications, changing system parameters or configuring security. People might have permission to customize their desktop a little, change the screen resolution and even perform updates to certain applications.

This is basically how it has worked for the last 20 years. With new versions of Windows, the resurgence of the Mac, more powerful PCs, the introduction of remote access capabilities, wireless networks, dual monitors, and a whole bunch of other additions, there has been a healthy amount of change in this area. In fact, there has been billions of dollars worth of change.

Companies are often using other technologies that also enter into the desktop mix, such as Server Based Computing / Session Virtualization, Software-as-a-Service (web applications) and virtual applications (all discussed later). Even if you have these technologies in place, your overall approach to the desktop and the people using them is probably quite traditional. The current solution is a desktop or laptop with installed applications, some common settings, and maybe a few Server Based Computing services, used to solve specific application issues that comprise the solution being offered.

For many people in your organization, this solution works relatively well. You are probably meeting many of the needs of the people that work in your company and they are generally happy with their PC, their applications, and the allowed limits on flexibility. When this is the case, time needs to be spent examining and considering how virtual desktops can provide an enhanced experience, or whether the implementation will be done as part of a straight replacement for the current solution. Virtual desktops have the ability to mimic the traditional setup, often in powerful and super-efficient ways that reduce total cost of ownership. Entire virtual desktop projects can be justified on this basis alone.

It was established earlier that people in your organization all have different technology needs. What is your understanding of their unique computer use characteristics? Does your IT department consider that some people are patient, while others are extremely impatient? Do some employees work at night, and others only 8 to 5? If your organization's technology staff addresses these characteristics, have the results been positive? Is your staff generally happy with IT?

If employees are not happy with the technology staff that administrates their desktops, it will be difficult to get participation for virtual desktop proof-of-concept and pilot activities. During the early stages of a project, the ability to test and collect feedback from the user community is an important element in achieving success. Because of this, it is imperative that you carefully consider virtual desktop use cases and the user population. If a particular user group is unfriendly or hostile to the project, consider different groups or approaches to improve the employee's experience with the technology. Examples might mean higher-touch service, careful selection of technical champions and detailed analysis of computer use characteristics.

Employees Have Standards

Computer use characteristics are most effectively addressed when considering the needs of the *employee*. As people, you might want to give everyone access to applications from home, but as employees, this presents too much of a security risk or the cost of support might be too high. As people, you want everyone to have a mobile phone they like using, but as employees, they all need to have Blackberries because that is the platform IT decided to use. You can see that by **abstracting** these groups of people to employees, you create the standards and rules around the technology they use to accomplish their goals, and often the ways in which they use it.

Some of these standards might be part of a user's or department's individual situation. For example, if users are given desktop PCs, it is unlikely they can take much, if any, of their work with them outside the office. There is a physical aspect to how an employee accesses and works with information that requires they be in the office. If the user does work remotely, it is likely because they are bringing data home on portable media or emailing it to themselves—both of which are likely violations of company policy. Other standards could be related to IT policy, such as the use of Windows 7 with the standard version of Microsoft Office 2010. Rules could be in place that state employees go through the PC lifecycle process and receive a new PC every 5 years. In some cases, rules and standards can directly affect the productivity of staff, create daily frustration, and even diminish morale.

This can easily be imagined in the case of a new CRM application that performs slowly and affects the outbound call rate of sales staff. If this application is deployed in the middle of the PC lifecycle policy, and nothing is done to address the problem, sales staff will be frustrated and actually earn less because their ability to process orders is compromised.

As you read this book, think about the different aspects of virtual desktop technologies and how they relate to the *people* working at your company. You should also consider how they relate to the *employees* working at your company. Once you have, get out and speak with your workers about their desktop solutions. What software is slow? Do they use dual monitors? Would they work from home if they had the opportunity? What kind of PC would they have if they could have any computer? Do they need access to areas of the Internet they can't currently use on their work PC? There are dozens of questions you need to ask to get an understanding of how virtual desktop technology will impact your users.

Chapter 3 will explain how to assess your current desktop environment using automated tools, but you also need to speak with users about the technology you are planning to implement. Consider end users the subject matter experts on the behavior of the desktop for their particular job. If you perform an automated assessment and speak directly with users, you are at the beginning stages of being informed. When you know what the standards for groups of employees are, and have spoken to different people in different groups to obtain a sense of the problems people currently have with their desktops, you can begin analyzing and making informed choices about virtual desktop technologies.

Now it's time to focus on one of the most fundamental questions of a virtual desktop deployment:

What happens to the people at this company when we change their primary work tool?

Answers to this question will vary drastically. If you take the path of a straight physical-to-virtual conversion for a user that sits at a desk, the user will experience minimal disruption. In the right conditions and with the right design, overall risk to the user when implementing a solution like that can be quite low.

The other extreme involves deconstructing the desktop into the essential applications, then making each piece completely self-contained so that they can operate on virtually any kind of device. Imagine a user wanting to access a very old application from a modern tablet device. Situations such as that are possible and it is often the case that business leaders are asking for, or at least contemplating, those kinds of capabilities.

Before making decisions about users, it is important to comprehend how virtual desktops can impact people at the most basic level. For example, with the right kinds of decisions, you have the potential to enable new ways to access information. With the wrong decisions, you can undo years of user training and expectation. As your company begins to work with desktop virtualization, it is critical that you realize there is a *person* using this technology as the primary tool to get his or her work done.

It doesn't matter if virtual desktops cost less or make IT more efficient if the change results in frustrated users, reductions in employee productivity, poor user experience or a slowdown in business.

Can that be said loudly enough?

Users are People Too

Understanding that users are people is especially critical for the IT staff, who often abstract people to a very general term: the *user*. Pools of people that use applications become generic and are spoken of in very general terms, sometimes with disdain or carelessness. A good example is the oft-confronted email quota. Email is a critical application to employees who need it to do their work. Some employees may send files to other users because it is easy, or keep lots of email because they refer back to it for information. It happens often enough that users sometimes run into what seems like an arbitrary quota and they can't send a file because there is not enough space in their mailbox. In order to send email, the users end up having to delete messages, some of which may be important, because they only get 500 MB of storage space, for example.

The technology team has hopefully established the quotas for a good reason, such as to keep the system operational and manageable. But in the above example, there is now a problem—the user cannot send an email because the attachment is too large and they don't have another way to transfer files. The user is having a poor experience and there is a resulting loss in productivity. Whose problem is this?

Some IT departments will address the users as people, understanding that this is a low-level incident and the user cannot send email, therefore they are not able to be productive. In this case, the result is likely some education and assistance, restoring the user to a productive state while keeping the quotas in place. Other technology staff may have difficulty handling a request like this, so it might be tagged as unimportant since it is "just a quota issue" and placed into the service request category. Even worse, some technical staff may arbitrarily decide to ignore company standards and remove the individual quota altogether.

Productivity is Key to Profitability

Think about how you would deal with a similar issue, except with virtual desktops. What happens when that administrative feature you thought was so great, like the ability to update an application on 1000 desktops with only three clicks, backfires and you lose an entire day of access to that application? The most immediate consequence is lost productivity and the impact it has on business. Imagine what it would be like without email or word processing for an entire day. With virtual desktops, a small problem with the infrastructure or applications can occasionally turn into a major problem, sending TCO calculations and company revenue in reverse.

Realistically, the IT department would probably test the application update before pushing the change into production. If the update resulted in a critical outage, the change could be removed with three more clicks. Maybe the application was only down for an hour and the company only lost a few hundred hours of productive time. But, this simple example does illustrate an important message that should be included in any discussion you have about all the great features—*virtual desktops can affect employees and worker productivity, and thus the bottom line.*

Always ask and be able to answer questions about how changes to virtual desktops affect employees and their productivity. Sometimes these changes can have a positive impact, such as users being able to work from home when there is inclement weather. Alternatively, performing system maintenance during peak system usage, while this action *supposedly* shouldn't cause any problems, might actually decrease performance of the system for all users. Updating a shortcut for all of the users at login can be performed at any time, so long as the change is tested and there is minimal risk of causing a problem. Sometimes large virtual desktop changes have little to no impact on end users, while at other times very small changes may affect thousands of virtual machines.

Virtual Desktops: A Real-World Example   The Vision

When talking about the effects of virtual desktops, the call center is an excellent example and does a good job of illustrating some of the benefits and challenges virtual desktops can provide groups of employees. Call center employees usually represent large groups of users concentrated in a few locations that may or may not be near the phone system. Today, many call centers are spread around the globe and their systems operate 24 hours a day.

Meet George. He runs a call center in a very tough business—*collections*. Prior to the implementation of virtual desktops in his company's three locations, employees had standard PCs. Client data was stored in the primary office building downtown, and the call center users' PCs worked well enough. The primary problem with their systems was that information wasn't secure enough for George's Fortune 500 clients. These are large, important clients that perform technical and data security audits with over 1,200 questions.

One of the main priorities for the IT department was to move their information to a more secure data center with the required processes and security in place. This project, with their complex call center software and continued use of regular desktop PCs, was cost prohibitive. The expense was due in large part to the type of infrastructure required between the office locations and the data center. Unfortunately, avoiding this high infrastructure cost was not an option because of how their primary line-of-business application worked. Switching applications was out of the question—too expensive and too disruptive to business.

The discussion about virtual desktops began when George was considering various technical solutions. If the information an employee was working on never left the data center, it would eliminate the high cost of infrastructure and secure the data to meet customer requirements. This is certainly something a virtual desktop deployment can accomplish.

> *Technical readers are thinking the perfect solution sounds a lot like Citrix XenApp or Microsoft Remote Desktop Services, or what is sometimes referred to as Session Virtualization (there is more information on this in Chapter 2). Without a doubt, that solution could be implemented to meet the security requirements and eliminate the high cost of connectivity. In many cases, it would be a satisfactory solution. But, if that was all there was to it, this would be a different book. Microsoft Remote Desktop Services and Citrix XenApp applications are very important components of virtual desktop deployments.*

Chapter 1: Sometimes users are just users

When discussing and comparing a traditional desktop versus a virtual desktop, George was intrigued by what he perceived as additional user and productivity benefits. In particular, when they were evaluating virtual desktop technology, George and his IT staff considered the effect the solution would have on their users.

The people working for George in collections are motivated by the volume of calls they can process. The more calls that each employee can service and the more clicks of the mouse that they do, the more money they make. That means there is a direct correlation between the earning potential of an employee, and thus the company, and the speed of the applications they use. If their applications are fast with only sub-second delays, it stands to reason that the most productive employees would be even *more* productive with the right virtual desktop solution.

George was very intrigued by this, as he could improve employee earning potential and productivity, while at the same time meeting the security requirements required by his clients. If the solution worked as advertised, virtual desktops would be perceived as a positive change by both management and the employees.

What else could a virtual desktop solution do for George's workers? George has three call centers. The primary call center is the largest, with two smaller offices in other metro areas. These offices have several groups of talented employees and future company leaders, but prior to the implementation of virtual desktops, office capabilities were limited by the centralized design of the technology infrastructure. Just like moving the line-of-business application to the data center would mean huge increases in infrastructure costs, serving the other offices with the same level of technology the central office used was an expense George could not justify.

With virtual desktops, George would be able to service users in the remote offices at exactly the same level as the central office. This would mean he could empower those leaders and workers with more responsibility and new initiatives to grow the business in those offices—all without any additional IT expense, extra personnel or special connectivity. The promise of virtual desktops meant that, in theory, George's business could expand to *any* metro area. More importantly, his staff could operate from anywhere his clients needed them to be. No longer would George just be meeting the security requirements of existing and potential Fortune 500 clients, virtual desktops would allow employees to serve those clients anywhere in the world with minimal investment in infrastructure and little to no change to existing processes.

After the Implementation   *The Reality*

Want to know what happened after George implemented virtual desktops for his collections business? What about his users? What about the other offices? After about a year, many of the benefits George thought the company would receive occurred. While the initial transition was quite smooth, there was a lot of fine tuning that had to be done to the system, and that was after a thorough proof-of-concept and pilot.

[Problem 1] At launch, applications on the new system performed very well. Users were quite surprised by the improvements in speed they experienced when compared to the older desktop systems. After several months of using the new system, George's company started to grow. George hired additional employees, which translated to more people using the virtual desktop system. This resulted in a noticeable decrease in performance, frustrating the other users of the system who were accustomed to applications operating at a fast speed. The employees had come to depend on that speed to get their job done. When things slowed down, the user's poor experience resulted in them having lower satisfaction and being able to do less work.

[Need Good metrics] The lesson for George was that while there were immediate gains in productivity, those gains were later negated by growing pains. While it was understood by technology staff that the employees depend on their virtual desktops to perform at a certain level, they had used "soft" metrics to determine and judge performance characteristics. The use of poorly defined metrics was fine when the system was fast, but when tasked with addressing the slowdown in application speed, IT was unable to accurately quantify the problem. When users called to complain, technical engineers only knew that the system was performing slowly and could offer no further help. Sometimes this was perceived by users as harsh treatment from the technology staff. If

that wasn't bad enough, management became aware of the problem when slow application performance began to cause collection rates to drop.

Solution — This problem did get solved, however, and ultimately in a very good fashion. By using specific, detailed metrics, the technology staff determined how to keep performance levels of the application within an acceptable range with the number of users on the system. IT leaders could now plan ahead when management informed them of new hires or changes in usage of their primary line-of-business application. They could scale their virtual desktop solution at a very fast rate without any significant problems. It was unfortunate their initial virtual desktop design did not address the need for well-defined performance metrics and the ability to scale out the solution to accommodate additional users.

Warning — Even with a good proof-of-concept and pilot, it is almost guaranteed that your IT department will still encounter challenges and growing pains after deploying a virtual desktop solution. These challenges can be complex and difficult to overcome, especially as you progress from a proof-of-concept of 50 users to a pilot of 500 and then a production system with 10,000 users and 14 different use cases. Scaling virtual desktop deployments should keep performance for the end user at an acceptable level.

> ***Keep employees productive, irrespective of any IT or project goals. If there are problems with the virtual desktop system, stop, solve the issues, and then move forward.***

The remote offices were a true success story for George's company. During the same year they were experiencing growing pains, one of the remote offices tripled in size. When the virtual desktop system was combined with an extension of the central phone system, technically no difference existed between an employee in the central office and one in a remote office. The result was better and more advanced service to the company's customers. And better service was not the only gain. The new technical capabilities at the remote offices translated into new opportunities for the employees at those offices.

The first opportunity was that users were able to be more productive. With virtual desktops, every application worked faster than it had before, resulting in a profound change for groups of employees that were used to feeling underserved by the IT systems. As IT and the remote locations became used to this arrangement, it gave the branch offices the ability to request improvements. IT was able to deliver these new and exciting changes quickly and easily with relatively little work. Overall, business at the remote locations became faster, more efficient and more stable.

The second, more profound change at the remote offices involved the people that worked there. Leaders working in the remote offices were given responsibilities that previously had to be performed within the central office. Now, no matter where a person worked, the right person could do any job from any location with the same tools as the central office. A local manager could hire five staff on Thursday and have the new employees report to work on Monday with brand new monitors and virtual desktops ready to go. IT didn't have to do anything to set up those new hires because non-technical staff in the remote offices had been trained to set up the virtual desktops and necessary hardware for new users. A process that typically took 2-3 weeks now takes only a few minutes.

Is Your Company Ready for Virtual Desktops?

Naysayers may claim that all of this could be possible without the use of virtual desktop technology, and they would be right. All of it is possible, *within certain limitations created by those kinds of solutions.* Part of the power and allure of virtual desktops is that the technologies behind them can accommodate so many different systems, applications and use cases. Quite often, virtual desktops can be implemented with minimal change to the end user's experience.

If implemented in the right way, virtual desktops can provide every person in a company with equal or better access to the primary tools used to do his or her job, while the business runs faster and IT becomes more efficient—all at the same time.

If virtual desktops are implemented incorrectly, employees will become frustrated and overall less productive. The ability to deconstruct a desktop into various disparate parts means that the parts can be put together in both good and bad configurations. For example, if the network connection is slow, mouse clicks and typing won't show up on the screen at the same speed as a normal desktop. Slow typing could be something that happens for several hundred people at one or more locations. Some applications may be very responsive and fast, while others are troublesome and unusable because they were deployed in the incorrect manner.

For virtual desktop solutions that are centralized, geography can be extremely important. If virtual desktops are operating in the data center, the device running the desktop is located some distance from a user's keyboard, mouse and screen. In many cases, virtual desktops will require that every keystroke, mouse movement and piece of visual information travel over the network.

An example of a real-life scenario is physically locating desktops in North America and serving them to users in Asia (or vice versa). The different services and software managing this communication for the user can be very good. In many applications, you can barely tell a difference between a virtual desktop and a real desktop.

The geographic nature of centralized virtual desktop technology has recently led to the development of a number of "acceleration" technologies you will look at when deploying virtual desktops. Some will be software that allows video and graphics to work very well over a virtual desktop, and others may enable full 3D graphics or operation over slower networks. These are developing technologies and it is recommended you proceed with caution. Test them with your users and gauge reaction. Never purchase or rely on one of these acceleration capabilities without testing it with your users during proof-of-concept. Assuming that "acceleration" will take care of slow video and keyboard problems for a virtual desktop is a dangerous and ignorant assumption.

When considering use cases and productivity gains with virtual desktops, you can be very bold with some of the choices you make. The physical desktop, and the infrastructure required to run it, can now be completely changed. With centralized solutions, reasonable connectivity can power large numbers of users. Client-side solutions can enable better management and support of mobile workers.

1. *Where would you locate departments if you could put them anywhere?*

2. *What kind of savings could you provide your organization if your staff worked from home full time?*

3. *Would you attract more qualified employees with the flexibility to work from anywhere? YES!*

When beginning a virtual desktop project, it is important to focus on and understand the needs of the *people, employees* and *users* working for your company. As people, it is critical that a virtual desktop solution meet their needs for usability. As employees, it is critical that the virtual desktop solution fit within the standards currently in place for corporate desktops. Enabling more flexibility within these standards can be a powerful driver for pursuing and implementing virtual desktops. IT leaders must understand that *users* are also people and employees. Project leaders and stakeholders should not make assumptions about the performance of a virtual desktop solution, nor about what is acceptable to the end user. At the end of the day, end users are the customers that determine how well a solution enables them to do their work.

Chapter 1: Sometimes users are just users

Chapter 2:
The Six-Legged Stool

Virtual desktops are a rapidly-evolving subset of Virtualization, the biggest change in the technology industry since the commercialization of the Internet. While this rapid evolution brings exciting new capabilities and improvements, it also means a lot of market hype, particularly in the communities focused on and around desktop virtualization. With new announcements out daily, the task to educate oneself about even the most basic virtual desktop technology can be overwhelming.

This chapter will introduce and illustrate the six major components of a virtual desktop solution:

1. OS Virtualization
2. Session Virtualization
3. Application Virtualization
4. Connection Broker
5. Client Access Devices
    a. Computers
    b. Thin Clients
    c. "Other" Technologies
6. User Data, Profiles and the User Persona

The following sections will explain these technologies in a way that is easy to understand, but keep in mind these are six individual components that are sometimes referred to by different terms, or bundled together as a packaged solution. There are as many variables as technologies.

For people new to the virtual desktop world, or for organizations under strict governance, this may cause a fair amount of "hair pulling" and make the technologies appear too new, too risky or lacking standardization. *Don't worry.* As you engage vendors and work with the individual technologies, there will be reference project roadmaps for implementation and lists of both requirements and compatibility.

Throughout this chapter there will be discussion about how these technologies combine and work together, so it's important to disconnect yourself from all previous conceptions of what a desktop is or is not. A desktop is not a machine that has Windows or Mac OS installed. In fact, it might not even require a computer at all. Right now you do not have a desktop—just a blank slate. Now, hold that thought as you read on. Are you ready?

OS Virtualization

In the simplest terms, OS virtualization is when you take an operating system — Microsoft Windows or Linux — and run it on top of an application called a *hypervisor*. For all intents and purposes, the operating system running on top of a hypervisor is the same as an operating system installed on a computer. Users log in to the operating system and use it much as they would a traditional PC.

Using a hypervisor has numerous advantages, but for the purpose of this discussion, the most significant is the fact that you can install the hypervisor on a server, then have 50 or more virtual OS instances running on top of the hypervisor. This configuration allows you to have all instances share the same equipment.

No matter how it is done, the end result of OS virtualization is that somewhere there is a copy of Windows (or another OS) running applications. In presentation and use, it will almost always be similar to a copy of Windows that runs on a PC or laptop. However there will be a lot of variation in the organization of the underlying technology.

Examples of variations include:

- how the user data is managed
- where the virtual instance is run
- what kind of protocol and/or device is used to access the operating system

One important note here is that virtual OS instances can be run in the data center and connected to a device at a user's desk, or they can be run on a PC or laptop. The latter configuration, a type of client-side

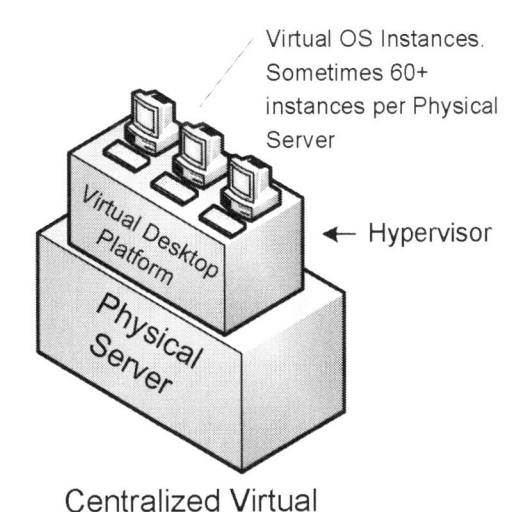

Virtual OS Instances.
Sometimes 60+
instances per Physical
Server

← Hypervisor

Centralized Virtual
Desktop Solution
(Many Physical Servers in the Data Center)

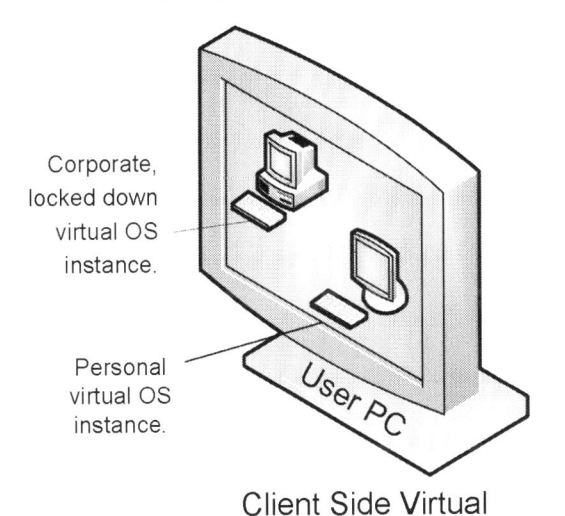

Corporate,
locked down
virtual OS
instance.

Personal
virtual OS
instance.

Client Side Virtual
Desktop Solution
(1 or more virtual OS instances per user PC)

Figure 2.1 — OS Virtualization

Chapter 2: The Six-Legged Stool

virtualization, adds new flexibility to the user's PC experience. For example, each user could have both a personal virtual OS and a company virtual OS. This would give the user the best of both worlds—lots of personal freedom *and* a locked down and secured corporate desktop. If you are a Mac user, you are likely already using a variation of this technology when you access PC applications through software like Parallels or VMware Fusion.

One of the most important distinctions of OS virtualization is how programs are installed and used. Outside of virtual applications and session virtualization (discussed later), applications are installed and used by one user—just like they are on a traditional PC. Session virtualization, the next technology presented in this chapter, is the foundation for session-based applications, in which one application installation is shared by tens or hundreds of users simultaneously (much like opening multiple versions of an application on your PC).

Session Virtualization

Session virtualization is the oldest, and likely the most familiar, of these technologies. It is also known as Terminal Services, Remote Desktop Services, Citrix, and a few other names. Citrix is the name of a company that originally built enhancements to Terminal Services and now has products spanning the entire world of virtualization.

Session virtualization is, in many ways, the opposite of a virtual OS instance. With session virtualization, a single server is enabled so it can share applications between 50, 200, 1000 or more people. Users log in to a remote system and can experience either a virtual desktop with a start menu and desktop, or a session-based application that looks and acts like an application installed on a PC.

A virtual desktop powered by session virtualization, a session-based desktop, means that users will see a remote desktop similar to a normal Windows operating system (start button, desktop, My Documents folder, etc.). It is important to note the word "similar" as *this is not the same thing as OS virtualization or an OS installed on a physical PC*. There are some very important advantages and disadvantages to remote desktops using session virtualization versus those using OS virtualization. One is not necessarily better than the other, but they do need to be thought of as being used for different things.

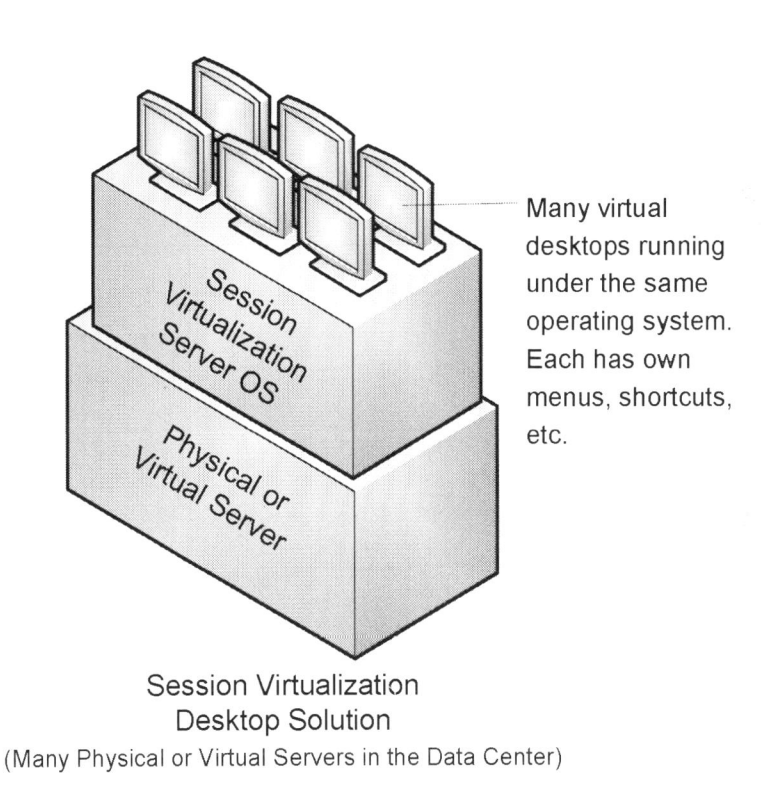

Session Virtualization
Desktop Solution
(Many Physical or Virtual Servers in the Data Center)

Many virtual desktops running under the same operating system. Each has own menus, shortcuts, etc.

Figure 2.2 — Session-based Virtual Desktops

There is a second type of session virtualization to address as well, and that is when an application is presented to a user as though it is installed on their desktop. Called a *session-based application*, the application appears and can be used almost exactly like an application installed on the machine. Many applications can be session-based and there are specific reasons for doing this.

The number one reason for access to session-based applications is for remote access, and is in fact why the technology was created. Another example would be when an application requires special computing resources in order to operate, such as very fast storage or large amounts of processing power. An application might need to reside very close to the database or application server that feeds it information. By publishing the application using session virtualization, users can utilize an application without needing any special hardware or software on their computer. It runs elsewhere so the user sees only the application's visual information.

While correct in concept, but not technology, it may help to think of session-based applications like many of the Internet applications you use every day. Think of Google. You are presented with a search box where you can enter a simple search term or a complex query. In effect, your browser is presenting the visual aspects of the application. When you enter information and press the search button, the information is sent back to Google, processed, and then you are presented with the results of your search. Your computer is not doing any work beyond simply rendering the visual information that the remote application has delivered. Session based applications work in a very similar way, just with nearly any application—even an Internet browser running Google.

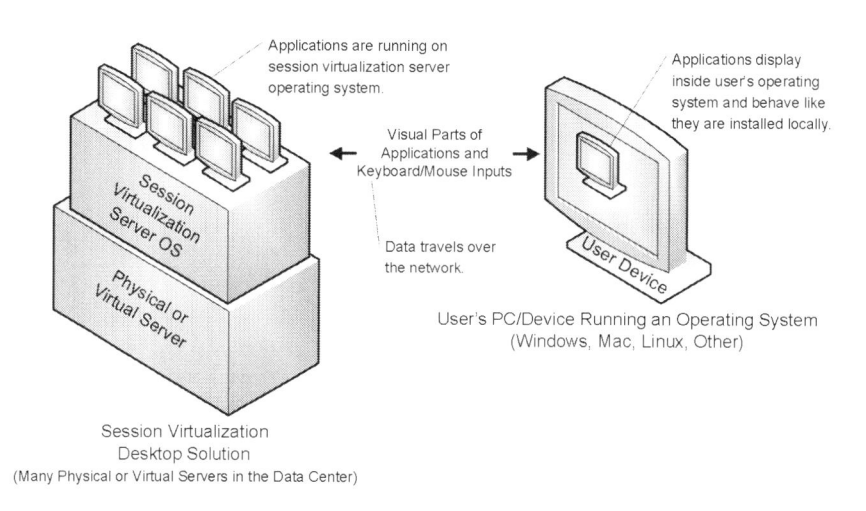

Figure 2.3 — Session-based Applications

Session-based applications can be nested and placed inside of OS Virtualization or session-based desktops. This means that you can take an application with special requirements and put it into a virtual desktop (or even a real desktop) like a puzzle piece. You can have the advantages of a virtual OS instance for one user use case, as well as the advantages of session-based desktops for another user use case, and provide them both with access to the same session-based application. The result is the best kind of desktop for the user use case, and the flexibility to use the same application in either instance.

You must think of virtual desktop solutions not as a single technology or software package, but instead as a combination of different technologies.

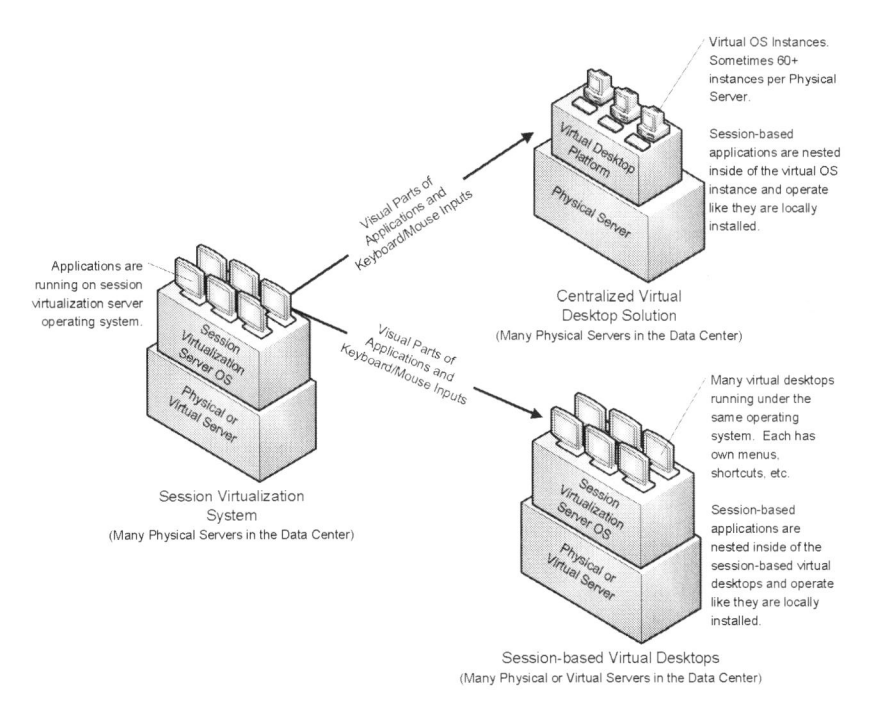

Figure 2.4 - Virtual Desktop Nesting Example

Application Virtualization

From an application standpoint, Application Virtualization has to be the antithesis to session-based applications. It is akin to comparing DaVinci to Michaelangelo. Their art is similar, yet completely different.

In a nutshell, application virtualization is like a present you would give someone. You buy the gift (your application) and put it in a box with wrapping paper on the outside (virtualizing it). You can then give it to someone and they can open it up and use what is inside. When put together in this way, virtual applications are called "application packages."

Essentially all application virtualization does is take an entire installed application and surround it by a virtual layer. When this happens, the application exists as one file a user clicks on to launch. It does not have to be installed, doesn't care which version of an OS it is running on and works on different kinds of devices—all within the limitations of the virtual application software, of course. Applications launch inside of a "bubble" and will have various levels of interaction with the OS they are running on. One virtual application may be setup so that it interacts in a limited fashion with the operating system and other applications, while another virtual application will be setup to completely isolate itself from the operating system and all other applications. In either case, once applications are made available, such as via a network location or web address, they are instantly available to users. *Unlike a session-based application, a virtual application uses the computing resources of the device that executes the application package. This device still may be remote from the use—such as in the case of virtual OS instances that are stored centrally.*

The reasons for virtualizing an application vary. One of the primary advantages of virtualized applications is the fact that, once packaged, they are separate from each other and the operating system. Separation of applications from one another and the operating system often has the advantage of eliminating conflicts that may exist between any number of software elements—items like OS updates, security patches, application dependencies or add-ins. Other advantages to the use of virtual applications are typically around compatibility, administration, distribution and licensing.

When considering compatibility, virtualizing an application might mean that older software can be made to run on newer operating systems, such as software designed for Windows 2000 that needs to run on Windows 7. When administrating applications, application packages generally come with methodologies and/or tools that can be used to centrally enforce licensing, software deployments, and package updates.

Warning! There are risks associated with application packaging. Virtualizing an application could violate software vendor license agreements (EULAs) or create a situation in which software can no longer be supported by the vendor. If you are unsure about whether software should be packaged, check with the vendor or a packaging expert to get their recommendations.

Earlier, the idea of nesting published applications inside of a virtual OS instance or a session-based desktop was mentioned. Of course, the same thing can be done with application virtualization. This is a very simple, but powerful piece of the virtual desktop puzzle. The solution for one user might be OS virtualization with a few basic applications installed on the OS, combined with some session-based applications and some virtual applications. For another user, you might just deploy the virtual application on their existing physical desktop.

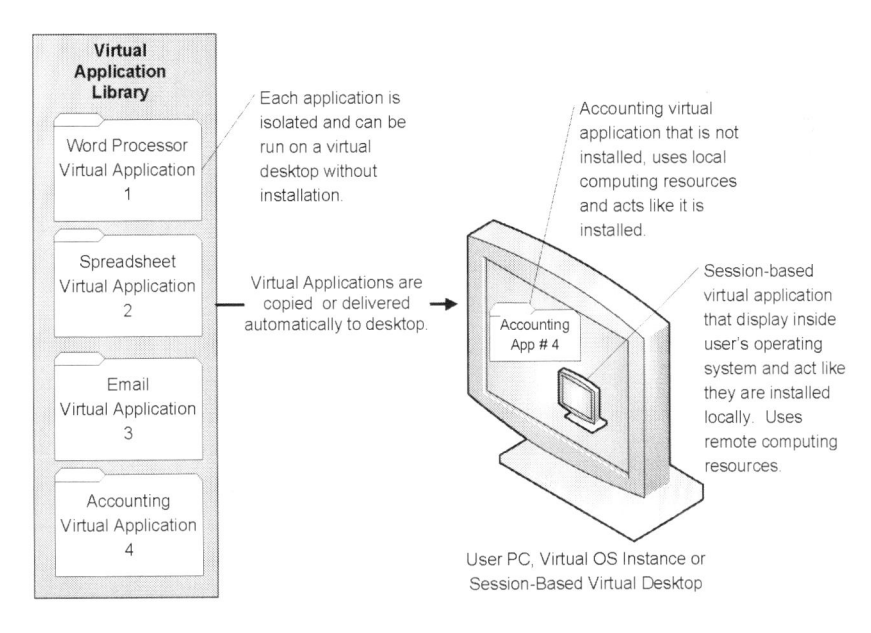

Figure 2.5 - Virtual Applications

Without a real system setup in a proof-of-concept configuration, it can often be confusing and frustrating trying to decide on the best way to combine technologies into a usable virtual desktop. Don't be surprised if the first combination or configuration doesn't work and you need to change it a few more times. You might not get it right at first, but over time you will gain experience and develop maturity in the use of these technologies. That maturity translates into an ability to effectively combine and use these different resources in the right way.

The Connection Broker

When you begin exploring the components of virtual desktop technology, the connection broker can be the most confusing, and sometimes the most difficult, to place a value on. Think of the connection broker as the doorman *and* the door that determines how and what kind of information is presented to a virtual desktop user. There are some connection brokers that are very flexible and have more options than a 7-series BMW. They allow you the ultimate in flexibility. You can control access to, and present a user with, any combination of the above technologies in any way, on any device, in any order, in any priority, with certain exceptions and certain service guarantees and special customizations and, and, and....get the point?

Oh, and this is all through one piece of software. There is certainly some security in having that level of flexibility, but this kind of software could have a steep learning curve for IT staff and require a larger upfront investment.

Other connection brokers are glossed over in the sales and technical material because they are more limited on features. They are designed to perform basic entry and exit functions with a few perks—nice and simple, and in a way, very elegant and user friendly.

Ultimately, the type of connection broker you use will come down to the immediate features you need, the kind of features you think you will need, and the overall cost of the solution. Some connection brokers are completely agnostic to the underlying technology and will use whatever virtual desktop technologies you choose, while others are tightly integrated into an overall virtual desktop product suite. The brokers that are a native feature of the virtual desktop platform you choose typically include the license fees in the licensing agreement, meaning that you are not purchasing another product.

A longer assessment of connection brokers is outside the focus of this book. They tend to undergo rapid development and vary widely on features. After you perform an assessment of your PCs and applications for virtual desktop consideration, list the minimum features you require from a connection broker. With this information, you can then analyze the features of the various connection brokers so that your purchase is driven by requirements and not the "extras" that they may include. The value of these extra features, such as increased flexibility, easier support, special protocols and the promise of future enhancements can then be examined knowing that the solution will meet all of your project requirements.

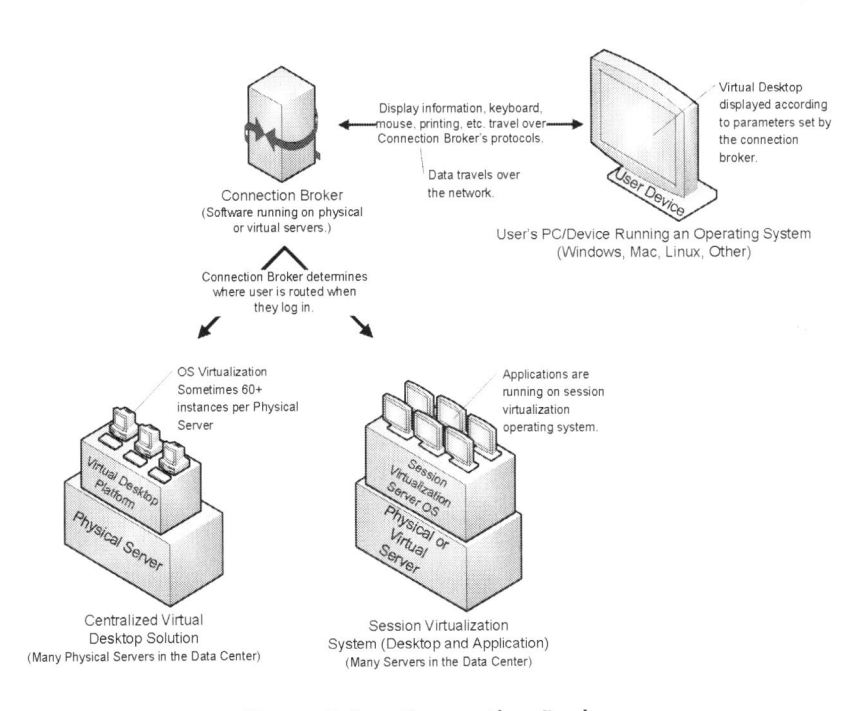

Figure 2.6 — Connection Broker

Client Access Devices

The second to last virtual desktop technology to discuss is the device used to access a virtual desktop. One of the best things about virtual desktop technologies is that they aim to be accessible by almost any kind of device running any kind of operating system.

Client access devices can be broken down into three categories:

- Computers
- Thin Clients and Zero Clients
- Smartphones and "Other" Technologies

Computers

In the case of a computer, there are two virtual desktop scenarios to understand. In one scenario, a computer running nearly any operating system can be used to access a virtual desktop, session-based application or virtual application that exists on a remote system. The installation of some type of client software is usually required in order for this to occur, but that software is typically small and requires a minimal amount of computing power. Sometimes that software can also be embedded into a web browser.

Because the system requirements for virtual desktop software are so low, organizations usually don't have to purchase new computers and can instead use their existing resources (often referred to as computer re-use). One caveat here is that organizations need to determine how they are going to manage these old PCs. To keep support costs down and improve the user experience, it might make sense to change the installed operating system or convert them into devices that can only access a virtual desktop.

There is a second scenario, called *client-side virtualization*. In this scenario a computer runs a virtual desktop (or set of virtual desktops) on a desktop or laptop computer. This is basically the same as providing your users with computers as you do now, then adding sophisticated virtual desktop technologies on top of that computer to ease administration and improve the overall operation of the PC. There are many different scenarios that make this a desirable configuration versus a traditional PC with an installed OS.

Thin Client Devices

As you begin researching virtual desktop technologies, you will hear a lot about thin client and zero client devices. In the case of thin clients, these are simply small computers without any moving parts, and they can provide numerous advantages over traditional PCs. Examples include longer replacement cycles, better manageability, and decreased power consumption. They typically have only one purpose in life: to access virtual desktops over the network.

Zero clients are devices that have even fewer parts than their thin client counterparts. There are a number of reasons that a company may wish to consider zero clients, such as for cost, specialty applications or enhanced security. Zero clients have many of the same benefits as thin clients and for the remainder of this book you can consider the two as synonymous with one another.

Because they don't have any moving parts, the lifespan of thin clients tends to be longer than traditional PCs. Thin clients also have the additional benefit of not requiring any installation expertise beyond the ability to hook up a monitor, keyboard and mouse. Most of their administration is performed centrally from a management tool provided by the thin client vendor.

Thin clients might be small, but they are still computers with optional functions and features that can increase their capabilities — *and their price*. For example, some thin clients support multiple monitors and sound, and have sophisticated management applications to control security and the end user experience. As vendors add features and increase performance, thin client devices are getting "fatter" all the time.

These advanced features make thin clients a *smart* choice to replace desktop PCs in a variety of use cases, but you might not know they are also a *green* choice. In addition to reducing overall support costs, thin clients can typically consume less than 10% of the power required to run a traditional desktop PC, lowering utility bills and benefiting the environment.

One last note about thin clients and computers is the hybrid solutions on the market. There are easy-to-configure software solutions available, some of which are open source, that turn PCs into thin client devices. While not as flashy and green as standalone thin clients, this approach can cost much less than replacing PCs with thin clients while still lowering desktop support expenses.

On the other end of the spectrum are "smart" clients. These are small, low-power PCs that fit in the market somewhere between a thin client and full computer. They can often run a full operating system and run applications locally like a typical PC, with many of the thin client benefits like manageability and lower power consumption.

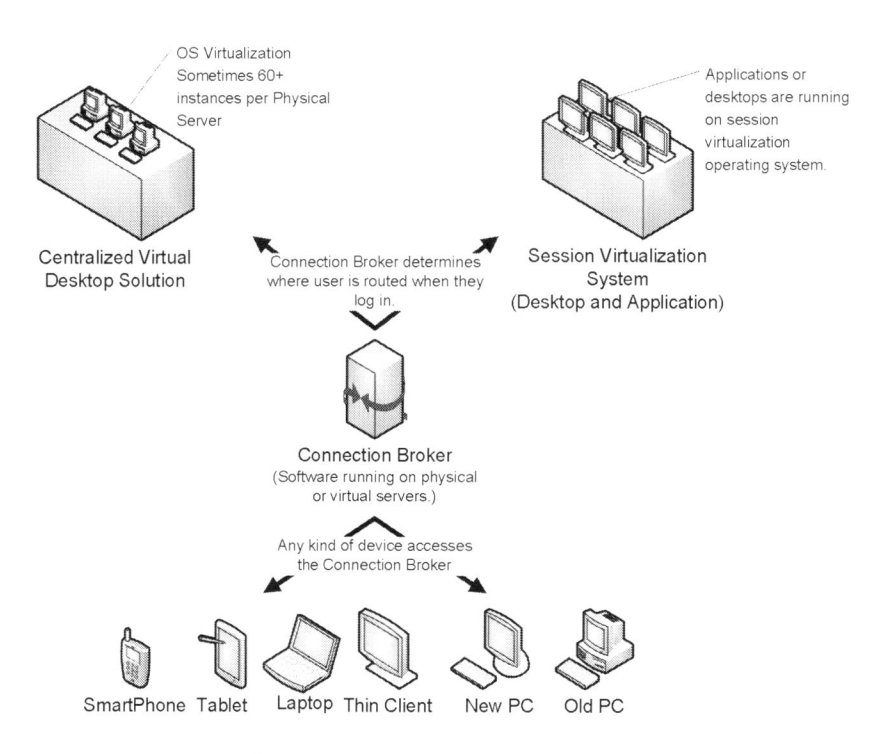

Figure 2.7 — Client Access Devices

Smartphones and "Other" Technologies

What technical discussion would be complete without the "other" category? Many devices and software solutions don't quite fit in either the computer or the thin client category.

Some devices are *almost* full computers, but they are modified in some way to make them more secure or more specialized for virtual desktops. Likewise, there are fancy thin client devices that can actually run software, play videos, and let users browse the Internet outside of the virtual desktop. Still others are tablet devices that integrate with special software and devices installed inside of the virtual desktop environment. Last are the 300+ million smartphones out in the world that are really just small computers.

The capability for users to view virtual desktops and to access applications is usually provided via software allowing users to view their virtual desktop from a web browser, a smartphone, tablet, or from a USB key they can plug into any computer. In the case of the most popular smartphones and tablets, this software is readily available on the online markets and users can often install and connect to their virtual desktop without any special help or assistance from an IT department.

Consider smartphones and the "other" category carefully when evaluating client-access devices for your virtual desktops. Specialized devices or software could be a great fit for niche applications or offer enhanced mobility that allows you to deploy virtual desktops in situations that couldn't function any other way.

Tablets are an especially interesting technology that can be used with desktop virtualization. Imagine for a moment executives that take their tablet into a meeting to access the same virtual desktop they were working on in their office. Since tablets can easily drive large monitors, it is not hard to imagine an executive pulling up reports and applications to collaborate with other decision makers in a conference room. The user data management application might detect that the virtual desktop has been transferred to a tablet that is being accessed from inside of the office and automatically add the conference room printers so that the executive can print material on demand during a meeting.

User Data, Profile Data and the User Persona

User Data, Profile Data and the User Persona are the very last components of virtual desktop technologies. User data consists of all the data files you access, such as spreadsheets and word processing files. Profile data is made up of customizations you make to applications and the operating system, such as special toolbar layouts and wallpapers. Other examples of profile data are Outlook account information and signatures, toolbar settings in MS Office, Internet favorites, recently-used documents, and all those handy desktop shortcuts. As it relates to virtual desktops, profile data can also be referred to as the user's "persona." When referred to in this context, the persona is the combination of user data + profile data being used by applications, the operating system, and an end user. Applications that perform this function might also refer to themselves as "personalization management," "persona management" or "profile management."

User and profile data is generally involved with three virtual desktop components—OS Virtualization, session virtualization and application virtualization. It is an integral part of the user experience and care needs to be taken with this information to ensure that it works properly within a virtual desktop solution. If you've ever lost your customizations because of a virus or computer crash, you know firsthand how devastating it can be. More importantly, user and profile data is often required information that a user needs to work with an application. For example, applications with custom dictionaries, special initialization files and toolbar settings often store information in the user or profile data areas.

The techniques used to manage user and profile data are complex and can vary significantly across virtual desktop solutions. While the technical details are far beyond the scope of this book, understand that there are two approaches to handling user data. The first involves the basic user data management features included with virtual desktop products and a Windows network. These two are used together to create the solution for user data management. The second approach involves the use of a third-party tool to manage the profile. These third-party tools include sophisticated profile management capabilities and can often ease the migration for users and administrators to virtual desktops and virtual applications.

Third-party tools are not necessarily better than those already included with the virtual desktop software you implement. These tools offer enhanced capabilities that more complex environments may require in order to function or scale correctly. The next chapter discusses the assessment of an existing desktop environment. Part of an assessment involves understanding the state of your user and profile data and applications. Once you understand this data, you can review and set up the right type of profile management system. Profile data can be quite complex within virtual desktop environments, especially as you consider the idea of "nesting" that is mentioned throughout these various technical sections. Using the built-in capabilities of a virtual desktop platform may mean that user data resides in multiple places, or that you must limit the ability for users to store customizations. Third-party tools generally break these kinds of barriers, ensuring that the user experience is more consistent and the management of user settings is easier for the virtual desktop administrator.

Chapter 3:
Desktop Assessments

Up to this point, you have read about the end user and their overall importance in desktop virtualization. You have also learned about the core components and technologies so you have a framework to reference when considering the various technical solutions in the market. Both of the previous chapters mentioned some of the ways your virtual desktop solution needs to be customized within your organization.

The next phases of understanding virtual desktop solutions, and how they might fit within your company, are virtual desktop *assessments* and *design analysis*. The assessments will summarize the state of your current desktops, users and applications. The design analysis contains all of the key elements of a virtual desktop deployment, allowing you to evaluate the overall impact of various solutions.

This chapter will walk you through the various parts of a general assessment and address, at a high level, the information that will be presented to you. As a technology or business decision maker for your company, there are two reasons it is important for you to understand and value a virtual desktop assessment. For the *technical* decision maker, assessment information is the only way to efficiently and accurately perform design analysis and create technical designs. Assessment information fed into design analysis provides valuable insight into the various technical solutions and their components. For the *business* decision maker, assessment information, when combined with a design analysis, provides an understanding of the business, staffing, management, and operational changes that might occur with the implementation of new technology.

Virtual desktop assessments and analysis models are linked together, and various pieces of information flow between the two and affect one another. This link suggests they should be addressed within the scope of a single chapter. But, because of the importance of these two tasks individually, and the ultimate value of virtual desktop design analysis, this part of the book has been split into two distinct chapters that overlap in some areas. This allows focus on, and simplification of, two very complex processes.

In practice, you might choose to follow this trend and split your assessment and design analysis into two distinct projects. If hiring a vendor to perform a virtual desktop assessment, both operations could be combined with an ultimate deliverable that is a solution recommendation. Merits to that approach exist and, in many cases, vendors will perform an extremely agnostic and thorough job.

It is important to double check the vendor's virtual desktop recommendations and design analysis to understand why they were applied in their solution recommendation.

Most times, the reasons to *not* implement one technology are as important as the reasons *to* implement another technology. This is especially true when working with a vendor that could be biased towards one type or brand of virtual desktop platform. They could simply be more skilled with one platform over another, making their recommendation not entirely appropriate or logical for you. If the solution recommendation doesn't already include it, ask the vendor to provide the list of reasons why you should not implement competitive technologies. This can be a simple litmus test that will help validate the vendor's recommendation.

The Value of Design Analysis

A *full* explanation of why you should customize the virtual desktop solution for your company will require you to read through this chapter and the next. But, to begin, you must first move past assessments for a moment and understand the general purpose of design analysis. Consider for a moment a virtual desktop recommendation that is presented to you. This recommendation indicates that virtual desktops will be less expensive than traditional desktops for your company, just like the marketing material said it would.

There is a vendor graph in the report showing a 45% difference between the total per-desktop cost of a physical desktop solution versus a virtual desktop solution. As you are examining the proposal, you remember hearing from a colleague at another company that they experienced no cost difference, while another shared that virtual desktops have actually been more expensive than regular desktops for his company.

Knowing this, how confident can you be that there really will be a 45% difference in the total per-desktop cost for your organization? The answer, "because the vendor knows what they are talking about," is not good enough. When making a decision about virtual desktop solutions, and especially when comparing different vendor recommendations, it is extremely important to understand in detail *why* a solution costs more or less. *Why* did your colleague at another company see no cost difference, but you are supposed to save 45% with desktop virtualization?

Answering the "why" questions illustrates the value of design analysis. By understanding the relationships between the high-level parts that make up your desktop computing solution, you can use that information to make quality, educated choices about the approach that is being recommended to you. As you read chapter four, you will be given a high-level framework that will allow you to question the way a design analysis is applied to areas such as physical infrastructure, staff, management processes and user access.

Consider that an important part in understanding the overall cost of any virtual desktop solution is the increase in resources you need to provide inside the data center. Implementing small numbers of desktops will likely have a negligible impact, but if you are planning several thousand, you need to understand the effect the new infrastructure will have on all areas of your data center, such as space, power, storage, servers and connectivity.

Virtual desktop design analysis will help you outline these costs and then understand the relationship that exists between all of the different elements. For example, a key relationship exists between your software choices and the physical resources you need to run that solution. Some configurations might provide you with very high densities (hundreds of users/server) that minimize data center costs. Others could have lower densities with higher operating costs, but include better management features that will ultimately reduce administrative expenses.

Considering system elements outside of the data center, do you know if it is more cost effective for you to re-use your existing computers as simple client-access devices, or should you replace those with low-power devices that are managed centrally? What if you just use client-side virtualization and don't put your desktops inside the data center? What if your company replaced corporate PCs with a device that your user chooses? What if they are also responsible for managing this device? In what ways will this be more efficient or cost less than a centralized solution?

Taken in context of your entire IT budget and the significant amount of change you can introduce by using virtual desktops, the analysis will allow you to improve the decision making process. Imagine a scenario where you are exploring virtual desktop technology to accomplish three things: aid migration to Windows 7, reduce support costs, and increase application reliability. With just those high-level goals and a project to virtualize enterprise desktops, you will be presented with questions about your data center, like:

- How much capacity do we have in our data center? If there isn't room to expand the data center, what kind of density do I need from centralized virtual desktop solutions?

- Is virtualizing user data and applications, and ultimately improving desktop administration and easing the migration to Windows 7, more important than moving the desktops into the data center?

- What kind of operating costs can we expect with virtual desktops in the data center? What if we just used client-side virtual desktops and kept management in the data center?

And this is just your data center! Most people considering an implementation of virtual desktops will be in a state of "not knowing what they don't know." The assessment and resulting design analysis will help you to "know what you don't know." By identifying weak areas, you can then investigate using tools, user interviews, proof-of-concepts, consultants, and technology guides to obtain the necessary information. This will give you a higher level of comfort and confidence to answer the question of *why* one virtual desktop approach is better than another for your company.

Why an Assessment?

As mentioned earlier, being able to answer the "why" questions begins with an assessment of your current applications, desktops, and users. How do you do this? A number of applications are available that perform many of the assessment tasks, and even some of the modeling tasks. The great thing is that these tools are specifically designed to consider all the major technologies outlined in chapter two.

Naturally, you want to know all about these great tools, right? Unfortunately, this is an area that changes so quickly that anything detailed in print here will surely be out of date within a few months. This information is easily available online and, even more importantly, this is a key area to discuss with vendors. Evaluating the toolsets a vendor uses for an assessment can be a valuable criterion for judging the accuracy, methods, and ultimate trustworthiness of their offerings.

For the rest of this chapter, it will be assumed you will use a consultancy to perform your overall desktop assessment. If you plan to perform the assessment in-house, by staffing your organization with experienced virtual desktop employees or by building this skill internally through training programs, the following sections will still be valuable to you.

The focus now is to provide you with a high-level overview of the assessment pieces, and to highlight some of the specific areas through the use of simple examples. This is not a comprehensive assessment approach — that will be provided by the software tools you use and the professionals you hire to perform this work.

Now that you have some understanding about the reasons for assessing and analyzing your current desktop environment, it's time to begin your assessment. Most assessment tools examine physical desktops, applications and users. Sticking with this organizational structure, the next section covers analysis of the physical aspects of your current desktop implementation, while the sections that follow discuss applications and users. Note that many of these subjects will be examined in more detail in the next chapter.

Physical Desktop Assessment

Most assessments begin with the physical aspects of your desktops — a hardware inventory and analysis covering components such as memory, CPU, power consumption, storage and network connectivity. This is an information-gathering exercise that involves a data collection system located somewhere on the company network and a set of agent software installed on the end user's PC. The agent software collects information and reports it back to the data collection system over a period of weeks. This data collection is benign and does not affect the user in any way. Two key types of measurements are involved in this information gathering—*total capacity* and *used capacity*.

Total capacity = the total computing capability of the group of users you are assessing

Used capacity = the total capacity actually being utilized

You will find used capacity of current desktop resources is often a fraction of total capacity, and some user types might have significantly higher used capacity than others. Because centralized virtual desktop solutions are typically designed to accommodate used capacity rather than total capacity, the accuracy of the used capacity numbers is extremely important. Some assessment tools can take over a month to gather enough information to provide accurate results.

For example, a finance group might be performing lots of data analysis tasks at month-end, meaning their used capacity of computing resources fluctuates drastically across a period of 32 days. Meanwhile, an admin group could have steady use of computing resources with no fluctuation in resource utilization during this same period.

When considering client-side virtual desktops, a significant difference might exist between the used and total capacity observed in your assessment versus what you plan for in the design phase. This difference can be accounted for by the change in use cases sometimes offered with client-side implementations.

For example, companies might offer their users a secure, locked-down corporate virtual desktop and a second virtual desktop for personal use. Across large numbers of users, significantly more computing resources are needed to run two virtual desktops per person than one. Used and total capacity information is still valuable though, as it helps you understand how to size the client-side virtual machines and the necessary types and quantity of hardware you need for each client end point.

Among both client-side and centralized implementations, the change to virtual desktops does not mean you plan to just meet the used capacity found in the assessment reports. There are other factors to consider as well, such as changes to applications using virtualization, or upgrades to newer operating systems that require more memory and storage. Many assessment software applications can assist you with accounting for these changes. Some have sophisticated capabilities to help you analyze what applications are the best candidates for virtualization, whereas others might even help you size the servers you need for a centralized virtual desktop deployment.

When analyzing desktop PC hardware, assessments will focus on three areas:

- Processor (CPU)
- Memory (RAM)
- Storage (Hard Drive)

It is important to understand the ways in which measurements of each of these three resources will be taken so you can interpret the results correctly.

- *How will CPU be reported to you after the assessment is complete?*

- *Is the measurement something you can easily translate into CPU in centralized deployments?*

- *With storage, how does the filtering work?*

- *Can you determine the amount of custom user data outside of application and operating system data?*

- *Do you know the level of storage activity (or IOPs) for the desktops and individual applications?*

Local Area Network (LAN) performance is another area assessments might include, though they are generally not of significant concern in regards to the overall process. Understanding LAN bandwidth usage for each desktop is important, but not necessarily critical to the decision-making and modeling process. There could be some increase in network usage when virtual applications are sent to physical desktops over the LAN, as well as with client-side hypervisors. In these cases, it is important to ensure end points have a healthy network with plenty of network capacity to the central locations where information is stored.

Connections to central locations, and the Wide Area Network (WAN) in general, should be examined in detail during the assessment phase. At the most basic level, you need to consider the following specific information: type, capacity, usage statistics, typical latency (a time measurement showing how long it takes for data to travel from one location to another along a data circuit) from the closest central location, service-level agreements and the cost of each circuit. Some assessment tools will analyze and collect useful information about the performance of your network. In order to assess all of the networking information, you should review network statistics and monitoring data from other sources, as well as involve qualified networking staff in your analysis and data gathering efforts.

WAN data and centralized virtual desktop deployments are very good examples of the fluid movement of information from assessment to design analysis mentioned earlier in this chapter. The assessment process should leave you with general indicators that will affect your virtual desktop design. For example, take a single location that is a candidate for centralized virtual desktops. A critical piece of technology that will be decided on during design analysis is the protocol used to transmit information to this candidate location. That protocol will have certain network requirements, such as capacity per user (network bandwidth), or a limit on the time it can take for information to travel to that location (network latency). In some cases, this protocol choice could require changes to your WAN to support virtual desktops.

When this information is placed in a design analysis, the overall effect and cost of these changes can now be understood in the context of all other variables being considered. If a certain protocol has too many requirements, it might lead to alternative technologies for that part of the design. This is a case where the assessment, and the resulting execution of a design analysis, can help you "know" about the WAN and protocol specifics. The design analysis will identify areas where you "don't know what you don't know" and prompt you to perform more research, or to revise a design so that you "know" the effects of choosing a specific protocol.

Another area to include as part of the physical assessment is the power consumption of your desktops. Some assessment tools will give you detailed consumption information, while others cannot. If your assessment tool provides the amount of time users are logged in and active, you can still use a simple power consumption equation to get this number.

To calculate the rate of consumption, multiply the total number of PCs and laptops by their average power consumption (150W for desktops/ 50W for laptops) then divide by 1000. For 500 desktops, this formula would be:

$$500 \text{ (PCs)} * 150W = 75,000W$$

Since electricity is actually billed in kilowatt hours (kWh), we would then divide by 1000 to convert this number to kWh.

$$75,000W \div 1000 = 75kWh$$

So, these 500 desktops use 75kWh of electricity. Multiply this by the average number of hours computers are powered up to get the total number of kilowatt hours for your location.

$$75kWh * 9 = 675kWh$$

Chapter 3: Desktop Assessments

Once you know the local kW/h rates of your utility service (these rates vary per site, of course), you can then estimate the monthly spend on power for desktop PCs. At 15 cents per kWh, this example would yield a cost of $3,000 per month to keep the PCs powered on for 9 hours a day. It would be more than double that amount if they were left on overnight.

Centralized deployments using thin client devices will use power and cooling inside the data center, causing a shift or addition in operating costs that you should be aware of. If you are considering computer re-use as part of a centralized virtual desktop deployment, don't forget to compare power savings offered by newer devices and account for the overall increase in power consumption you will add to your annual expenses. For some companies, power consumption can be a six-figure annual cost. Since thin clients use less than 10% of the power required by PCs, they could be a better option than computer re-use. When using computer re-use along with centralized deployments, it is essential to understand the addition of equipment inside the data center will result in a *net gain* of power consumption.

Once you have researched your power consumption and all other physical components have been assessed, you will be well-prepared to perform much of the virtual desktop design and solution analysis. Hopefully you now have a sense for the complexities of virtual desktop assessments, and are beginning to consider how to perform one in your own company.

Application Assessment

The two remaining areas of the virtual desktop assessment process pertain to *applications* and *users.* Unfortunately, these areas also involve different kinds of data and are no less complicated than the physical portion. Since they are open to some level of interpretation, there is always the possibility the information produced during the assessment will be less accurate than the data collected by the assessment software. Whether this is performed internally or by an outside vendor, be very careful with application and user analysis. You should ensure input comes from the people in your company with the most intimate knowledge of users and their applications.

Automated assessment tools provide a lot of information about user habits, such as when they begin working on their desktops in the morning, what applications they use, and whether or not those applications are good candidates for application virtualization. Many will even give you user performance information, such as how long it takes for an application to start. This information is useful during all the phases of a project, from assessment through delivery and management. For example, comparing application launch times before and after implementation can help you determine if virtual applications start up more quickly than installed applications, allowing you to quantify the improvement in user experience.

As you go through the process of virtual desktop assessment and design, consider the starting points for virtual desktop implementation. The logical approach is to begin with assessment, perform the design, move on to proof-of-concept and/or proof-of-technology, then pilot and transition to implementation. Most virtual desktop solutions will use some quantity of virtual applications because their use affects the quality of the design and implementation. Implementing virtual applications before transitioning to virtual desktops can generally be a more desirable approach for some companies.

Many people reading this could already be using application virtualization to some extent. In that case, the information from the virtual desktop assessment should be used to consider a more complete use of the technology, ultimately easing the transition of your traditional desktops to their virtual counterparts. It might mean you implement this technology with your current workstations (both with and without the use of centralized or client-side virtual desktop infrastructure), resulting in a set of hybrid physical desktops.

Implementation aside, an application assessment will include information from three areas:

- Automated tools
- Application support costs
- Licensing costs

Obtaining this data might require you to compile a lot of information from disparate and potentially difficult sources. Of course, the more detailed and accurate the information, the better the corresponding assessment and design analysis will be. Understand that in addition to the information provided to you by automated tools, you will probably be forced to come up with estimates or SWAGs (Scientific Wild Ass Guesses) for some of the information you will need.

The information you put together most likely won't be exact, but it should be as comprehensive as possible. It will also help if you are aware of the weaknesses in your data; not necessarily to fix them, but to identify potential risks so you can work towards mitigating them in your design analysis.

Automated assessment software will provide you with a shortlist of applications and the potential for them to be virtualized. It will also give you a complete inventory of applications in use among a specific user group, as well as which applications are installed but not used. One piece of complementary information the assessment tools are not able to provide is the cost of support for individual applications. Even if you can only estimate these costs, those with the highest numbers should go on your shortlist as candidates for application or session virtualization.

Application or session virtualization does not necessarily require a full virtual desktop infrastructure, thus supporting the approach of addressing applications first to realize more immediate benefits and ease the overall transition to a complete virtual desktop implementation. As you compile this information and consider this approach, it can be valuable to separate support costs into percentages you can attribute to physical problems, application problems, and operating system problems. If you are really serious (or detailed/persistent/creative), you will create support cost estimates or scores for each individual desktop application and component.

During the assessment phase, it is important to consider the reasons for support of applications. If there are problems with the servers running these applications, or if they are difficult to use and have a lot of bugs, application or session virtualization probably won't improve application reliability or lower support costs. In addition, some applications may not virtualize well because of dependencies or other unique attributes. This is a perfect example of why it is so important to review your list of candidates for application virtualization with support staff, network administrators and expert end users. This allows you to confirm the app is a *qualified* candidate and to note any special user or technical considerations.

The third, and final, piece of information to gather during the application assessment phase is licensing costs. Assessment tools should show you *installed* versus *used* applications. This data, combined with the use of virtual desktop technology that delivers applications only when a user uses them, could reduce application license costs for your organization. This cost reduction can happen in a number of ways, such as the removal of assigned licenses from users that do not actually use applications. Do not make assumptions about licensing - pay specific attention to the details of the end user license agreements (EULAs). For example, some EULAs that operate on the *named user* model state that a license is assigned for a minimum period of 90 days.

As you consider application migration and upgrades, examine license issues closely with application vendors to assess any impact application virtualization and session virtualization will have to the cost of software upgrades or annual maintenance expense. Some vendors actually charge differently for applications running on virtual desktops! In addition, application virtualization can limit or eliminate vendor support for specific applications.

Because application assessment costs consist of support costs, license costs, and virtualization possibilities, the overall considerations outlined in this section make this portion of the assessment seem relatively easy. It is easy — on an *individual* application basis. It becomes far more difficult when you begin to look at *all* of the applications in a company. Just think about doing this for 200, 500, or even 5,000 different applications.

What if your company doesn't have, or can't produce, a full application inventory? Repeating this process for each individual application will be extremely difficult and you might be forced to group applications together, limit the total scope of applications you evaluate, or rely primarily on information provided by automated assessment tools.

These real-world adjustments are entirely acceptable, as long as you identify and state the potential risks that might be involved by limiting your application analysis. The lack of analysis can then be accounted for in the design analysis, allowing you to see the overall risks of an individual solution, approach or technology.

A good example of this is the comparison of centralized virtual desktop technologies to client-side technologies in an application's visual performance. Centralized technologies involve a network and connection protocol component that has an effect on the visual performance of an application. This generally doesn't need to be considered in client-side virtual desktop implementations; therefore, the design analysis will have a different set of risks when you consider the visual performance of certain applications.

Specific risks of virtual desktop technologies and approaches will either affect the *users* and their productivity, or affect the *centralized systems* and their reliability, scalability and performance. The risks affecting the users might be acceptable as potential system limitations, or mitigated through processes or technical design changes. As you go through the assessment and are gathering all kinds of data about the physical systems and applications, refer back to chapter one and refresh your memory of why user productivity and satisfaction are also important.

User Assessment

The primary purpose of the assessment, in regards to your users, is to summarize the information about their current experience so you have a foundation to design a comparable, and hopefully better, solution. Some assessment tools will go to great lengths to quantify the user experience into something you can score. Many will even provide a way to compare data before and during a proof-of-concept to show acceptable performance. While this quantitative data is valuable, it should not be taken as the only means of ensuring user satisfaction and system performance.

If you think back to the example of George's call center from chapter one, remember the users that grew frustrated as business expanded and the virtual desktop system slowed down? While that example demonstrates the need for constant monitoring of performance after implementation, it is not something that would have shown up in an assessment, or even a proof-of-concept. The experience the users had in the proof-of-concept was that the system was much faster than what they were used to. What if the reverse happened to you? What if you quantified a user's tolerance during your assessment then put a test solution in front of them and they became frustrated, or you calculated a reduction in productivity?

Assessing the current user state and experience is a difficult task. Even with tools to aid in quantifying this information during the assessment phase, be sure to include hands-on work that involves speaking with end users, supervisors and business unit leaders. Consider them the subject matter experts in the overall user experience of the desktops and applications. Value their input and use it in addition to what you gather through technical analysis.

As you move to the next chapter, and the next phase of your virtual desktop journey, you will begin to design and compare different solutions through the design analysis process. Your physical desktop assessments will translate into the physical needs for your new solutions. Your application and user assessments will determine the actual technology the end users, leaders, and application administrators work with on a daily basis, and how these solutions will affect your support staff.

Your physical, application, and user assessments are critical to the overall success of your virtual desktop design. In addition to the use of automated tools, it is essential you speak with and engage end users and leaders in face-to-face conversations. Without a quality assessment, you are building a virtual desktop target state without a source. Ultimately, the better your assessment, the better your ability to compare different solutions, understand key areas of risk, and progress towards a state in which you "know" the right solution from the wrong one.

Chapter 4:
Design Analysis for Virtual Desktop Solutions

In chapter three, you learned about the assessment phase of a virtual desktop initiative. You also saw numerous references to the design analysis process, which will be examined in detail in this chapter. Design analysis is important because it is the point at which you and your organization begin to make decisions about desktop virtualization. These decisions impact the entire company, from the end users and their productivity to the IT teams and the skills they need to do their jobs. These decisions also dramatically affect how much a virtual desktop project is going to cost.

Before beginning a design analysis, it is helpful to understand exactly what the process is and how it should be used in a virtual desktop project. Design analysis is not a formal, well-defined operation. Depending on the methodologies of your company or vendors there may be variations to the process, such as if your company's IT governance and budgeting requires that new projects be defined in a specific way. The rest of this chapter will provide you with a high-level framework, similar to the assessment sections, by touching upon the six most significant areas to consider when performing a design analysis. This straw man framework will need to be modified to meet the needs to your organization.

The components covered in design analysis are:

1. Design Analysis Components
2. Centralized Physical Resources
3. Virtual Desktop Platform
4. Administration
5. Applications
6. Client Access

As you explore virtual desktop technologies, vendors, and the plethora of educational marketing material available, you will find a number of approaches to get from assessment to deployment. These approaches often involve design, proof-of-concept, and pilot stages as the middle ground between assessment and full production. Design analysis is a two-part substep of the overall design process and serves two primary functions.

The first function is the **assessment analysis**, where you will review, consider and document assessment information. Once this has been completed, you will enter the design phase, and you might encounter a loop until assessment analysis is refined by the design team.

The second function is the **design analysis**, which occurs *after* design and examines all of the design requirements, configurations and costs. There will be a second loop that exists during design analysis in which the quantitative results of the analysis change the design. An overview of the process looks like this:

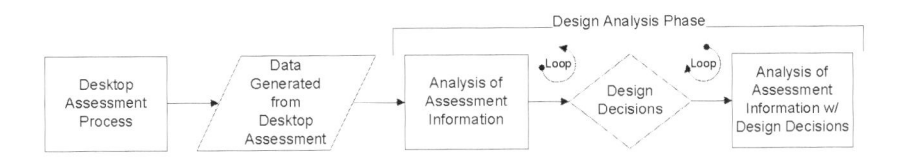

Figure 4.1 — Design Analysis Process

Assessment analysis has the most value when conducted right after the assessment phase. Ideally, information from the assessment analysis is put into a design, and then design information is graduated into the design analysis. If you want to be even more thorough, once you have gone through this process, the documents and models can then be used to help improve design during proof-of-concept.

A design analysis is a physical set of documents and spreadsheets representing the information you are working with. Since the primary audience of this book consists of technical and business decision makers with various skill levels, the processes outlined below will focus on the creation of the design analysis using just a small set of documents and a single spreadsheet.

Design Analysis Components

A simple virtual desktop design analysis requires you to create three sets of documents:

1. Requirements documents (lists project requirements)
2. Design documents (describes the solution)
3. Cost model spreadsheet (shows how the two sets of documents and assessment information are linked together)

The sequential process of creating these documents will be:

1. Summarize assessment information
2. Create requirements documents
3. Designing for the requirements
4. Model and refine the design with the cost model spreadsheet

Once the assessment information is summarized and the requirements documents are complete, there might be conditions of design in which the team needs to know X or Y, requiring assessment information to be examined in more detail, or new data to be obtained. Once the design documents and the first cost model are complete, you will likely generate a refined cost model as you prepare and complete the proof-of-concept and proof-of-technology phases.

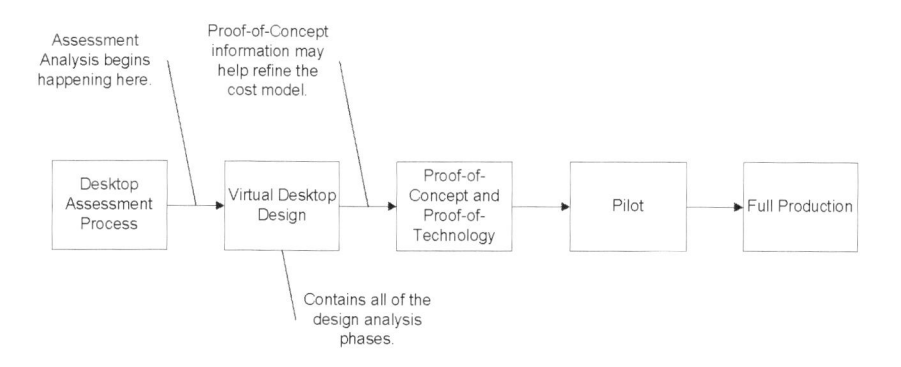

Figure 4.2 — In the Big Picture

Chapter 4: Design Analysis 63

The design document of a virtual desktop solution is typically a technical undertaking and will involve technical staff, consultants and vendors. Similar in scope to other design documents you have seen or created, it will address the requirements and problems of your virtual desktop project with documented solutions. Because of the technical nature of a design document, this chapter will not be a step-by-step guide on how to create one. Instead, it will prepare you for the task of creation and cover some of the ways in which the requirements documents and cost models are used with a design document.

The documents describing your project requirements are used in the technical design *and* in the creation of a cost model. The purpose of the cost model is twofold. First, it links project requirements to design. Second, it allows the design to be quantified so that important relationships can be identified and understood. *A cost model is simply a spreadsheet that outlines the numerical relationships between all of the disparate parts of a project.*

The cost model spreadsheet should include numerical values as functions of assessment information, requirements and vendor information and will automatically update when requirements, problems, or design elements are changed.

For example, the total number of servers needed to host desktops in the data center can be represented as a function of:

Total Number of Users / Recommended Users per Machine

or

Assessment Information / Vendor Information

In a real model, a more complex formula is used that considers many of the variables required to make an estimate, such as types of users (low/medium/intense usage) or hardware limiting factors (total memory/processors). This information will be quite useful, calculating requirements like how many servers you should have or how much power you will use, and it can also help you accurately outline and compare the estimated capital and operational costs of various technical designs.

Requirements Documents

There are three types of requirements documents:

1. Business Process Impact Analysis
2. End User Scenarios Analysis
3. Requirements Document

Business Process Impact Analysis

The business process impact analysis describes the core business processes that will be impacted by virtual desktop technology. It may or may not describe how these processes are going to change. Since many of these will be technical processes, generation of these documents should involve technology staff.

End User Scenarios Analysis

The end user scenarios analysis is simply a collection of use cases describing how the system is currently used by the end users. These documents may or may not include the future state description of how the user is going to use the new system. If it does include future states, be sure both the technical use cases and the business use cases for the future state are included. Technical use cases are descriptions of the technical events occurring when end users use a system, while business use cases are non-technical descriptions from the user's point of view.

Requirements Document

The requirements document lists a set of *testable* statements which describe the exact requirements that a design and production system must fulfill. These requirements will include individual statements like "each user will have a minimum of 30 GB of personal disk space" or "the system will allow for 1,500 concurrent connections," and they should be verified at the end of the project.

Some implementations might have a significant number of requirements. Do not focus on the actual number of requirements, but instead on making sure the requirements document is complete and thorough. As you move through design, proof-of-concept, and pilot phases, do not be reluctant about amending these documents if the original requirements or design has changed.

Document Scope

There is value in keeping your design analysis as simple as possible. *Simple* is a relative term, of course, so it is up to you and your team to decide what level of effort and detail is necessary and appropriate. In large part, the level of effort will be dictated by the scope of your virtual desktop assessment. If you assessed a large number of users with different types of desktops and applications, then you will need a more complex and detailed analysis. No matter how many users you assess, you still need to perform a complete and thorough design analysis.

The information you gain from your assessment should allow you to fully describe the business processes, user use case scenarios, and requirements. An easy way to start using the information from your assessment is to turn it into simple statements and requirements and then categorize those requirements into one of three buckets:

1. Describe the business process and how it will change.

   For example: Hiring a new employee requires a PC to be imaged and assigned to a user. Using a virtual desktop solution, new employees only need to be assigned to the correct virtual desktop pool and be given a thin client device.

2. Describe the end user scenarios with problems they may encounter.

   For example: Sales users are highly mobile and require laptops with applications and offline access. Therefore, they are not candidates for a centralized virtual desktop solution unless it has offline capabilities.

3. Describe the requirements of your solution in one sentence.

   For example: The solution will use existing data center capacity in Chicago and Sao Paulo.

Not all information from your assessment will translate into business process or end user scenarios. Instead, a lot of it will translate directly into requirements. Once you complete these first three documents, you have a set of problems and requirements the design team must then address and present with solutions documented in design documents. The solutions outlined in the design documents are then put into the cost model, quantifying the design decisions and helping you understand design relationships and overall project costs.

As mentioned earlier, once you complete design and begin the proof-of-concept phases, you can choose to keep or discard the design documents. As you go through the next half of this chapter, think of the design documents as a series of living documents you modify after each critical phase of your virtual desktop initiative. Keeping and using the design documents in this way will improve each successive or iterative phase of the virtual desktop process by:

1. adding problems that were previously unaccounted for in design,
2. adjusting for unknowns in design, and
3. allowing more accurate understanding and forecasting of project costs.

The willingness or capabilities of business and technical leadership to even perform a design analysis could vary considerably. The amount of work and results may seem undervalued amid any number of other real-world pressures. The next part of this chapter will help you understand the relationships between various virtual desktop technologies through a simple outline of the design analysis process. Hopefully this is proof that, even among those real-world pressures, going through the design analysis process results in a higher-quality solution, better team consensus, and a reduction in overall risk — all critical to the success of any major project.

As described at the beginning of this chapter, it is easiest to group analysis at the high level by using five analysis categories:

1. Centralized Physical Resources
2. Virtual Desktop Platform
3. Administration
4. Applications
5. Client Access

All the information you collect during assessments will roll up into one of these five categories. These are used for overall grouping and do not represent isolated components. It is important to realize the decisions you make in one category will affect all of the other categories.

Because all five categories are involved in all of the documents, it might be better to start with the areas most familiar to you and the easiest to complete. As you begin to fill out sections of the cost model spreadsheet, a picture will begin to form in your mind, making it easier to comprehend and address all of the unknowns. If you have an unknown, don't stop building your model — just mark the content as unknown and continue. Unknown elements can be summarized and represent the weakest portions of your overall analysis. This is good information to have! Once you know where the weaknesses are, you can clarify these items one at a time through a process of exploration, discovery, reassessment and/or experimentation.

The sections below discuss each of the five top-level categories, beginning with the physical resources and working through to the client-access device that sits right in front of the user. In a way, you could say it moves sequentially from the power plug in the data center to the keyboard at the user's workstation. This outline is for assessment and design information and is primarily within the scope of the cost model spreadsheet, with secondary consideration given to the rest of the document set. The graphic below shows how the data is mapped and referenced in use within the cost model spreadsheet.

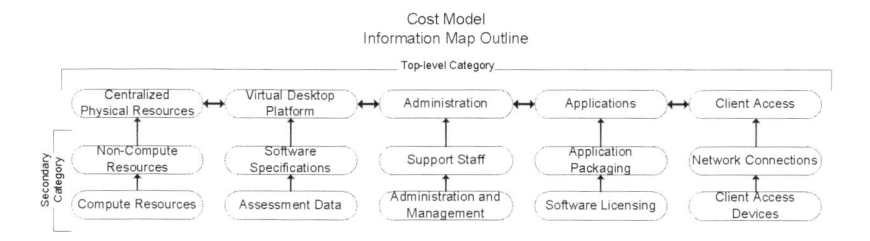

Figure 4.3 — Cost Model Information Map Outline

Centralized Physical Resources

Your virtual desktop cost model includes two high-level physical categories. The first involves the centralized, *non-computing physical resources* a proposed solution will consume. These are items like power, bandwidth, rack space and cooling, which are the same basic resources any centralized solution operating within a data center uses. The second category accounts for the *physical computing resources*. These items are the physical systems like storage and servers that consume power, bandwidth, rack space and cooling.

Together, these two high-level categories will contain very important numbers and will vary significantly depending on the solutions you choose for the virtual desktop platform, administration, application and client access categories. One way you might approach this is to think, "If we pick virtual desktop software A, then we need B computer hardware which consumes C power and needs D cooling." But, when doing an assessment analysis, that is the wrong approach. You first need to generate some additional data center requirements to use in design, and then place those into the cost model and design document set.

In order to generate the first set of requirements, you should classify centralized physical resources as potential constraints. Consider how much space and power are available in your data centers right now.

- *Do you have forecasts for data center capacity at 12 and 24 months out?*
- *Do these forecasts consider a centralized virtual desktop deployment?*

Chapter 4: Design Analysis

- Is there extra capacity inside of your data center for power or cooling?
- Are you colocating or leasing wholesale data center space?
    - If so, do you understand the constraints that exist around expansion, power costs and potential rate increases at your facilities?

Understanding the capacity of your data center as a resource constraint will allow you to generate a useful set of requirements for the virtual desktop design. Imagine you purchase a centralized virtual desktop solution without considering data center capacity.

Here are three potential scenarios:

1. Your data center has lots of extra capacity and everything will be fine.

    Consequences: None.

2. Your data center has a little extra capacity but will require some kind of expansion. *Consequences:* you start your virtual desktop project, encounter a five to seven-figure expense that comes out of someone's budget and adds 2 to 18 months of delays on projects requiring new hardware in that location (might not be just your virtual desktop project).

3. Your data center has very little extra capacity.

    Consequences: you just spent money on software licenses and hardware you can't even deploy.

Pay special attention to the user density a centralized solution will support. Once you have completed a design, refine the cost model spreadsheet to calculate exactly how much of the available resources a particular solution is going to consume and cost in data center operational expenses. By doing this you can be assured that:

1. The proposed solution will not consume more data center capacity than is available.
2. The proposed solution's data center operational expense will fit within the allocated budget.

3. You can truly compare more than one virtual desktop solution on the merits of total cost attributed to capital and operational expenses inside the data center.

Once you have incorporated the quantity of available resources within the data center, the next step is to set up the calculations to outline the total number of servers and storage equipment you will need for a design. Once you have a design that fulfills those requirements, you can complete the calculations to determine the quantities and types of physical computing resources you need.

The final design document should contain the recommended hardware configurations. That information can then be put into the cost model spreadsheet as formulas which relate design requirements to the resources each server will consume — thus linking all of this information together.

Calculations in the areas of hardware capital expenses and operational expenses, like power and cooling usage, will help you understand the true cost of a design. Use this information to compare different solutions and make further refinements to the design. Once complete, the information can also be taken into proof-of-concept to validate the assumptions and estimates.

Good starting points to begin the Centralized Physical Resources portion of your design analysis:

1. Understand current data center load and availability of consumable resources like power, space and cooling.
2. Consider your ability to accurately forecast data center capacity, including virtualized desktops.
3. Compare a centralized virtual desktop solution to a client-side solution, which requires fewer data center resources.
4. List each available physical resource a centralized virtual desktop solution can consume as a requirement.
5. Consider geographic and/or hardware technology limitations currently inside your data centers, such as storage or server types, as potential requirements.

Chapter 4: Design Analysis

Virtual Desktop Platform

Have you thought about how you are going to choose a virtual desktop software platform? Maybe you are going to evaluate the three leading solutions and see how and where they can be used within different user groups. Alternatively, maybe you are open to less mainstream technologies that make extremely efficient use of centralized resources.

- *Will you need more than one virtual desktop model for different business units and/or user requirements?*
- *Are you only considering client-side virtual desktops and won't need to worry about centralized resources?*

A design analysis will influence your package selection process by helping you state required features the design must address. At the same time, it will help you determine the total cost of a given solution. In reality, technical and administrative features, as well as vendors, will steer you away from a selection based purely on requirements and cost. It is thus important to modify this design analysis framework to include additional requirements from your overall package selection criteria.

Much like the centralized physical resources category, this portion of your design analysis will have value during the assessment analysis, but most of the benefit comes from the ability to analyze a design through the cost model.

First, the spreadsheet should contain all of the relevant and useful numbers from your assessment, such as how many users you have, how often they are using their PCs, CPU and memory needs, etc. Most of this assessment information can be translated directly into requirements for use in your design. As shown in Figure 4.3, once you have a completed design, you can insert the relevant software specifications and costs into the spreadsheet, transferring the cost of the software your organization will use into a format that can be analyzed.

```
┌──────────┐   ╱Data      ╱   ┌──────────┐   ┌──────────┐
│ Desktop  │  ╱ Generated╱    │Analysis of│  │Data Entered│
│Assessment│─▶╱   from   ╱───▶│Assessment │─▶│in Cost Model│
│ Process  │ ╱  Desktop ╱     │Information│  │ Spreadsheet │
└──────────┘╱ Assessment╱     └──────────┘   └──────────┘
```

Example Assessment Data	
Total # Users:	1346
Total CPU Required (MIPS):	89,388
Total Memory Required (GB)	3600

→ Insert Software Specifications During Design

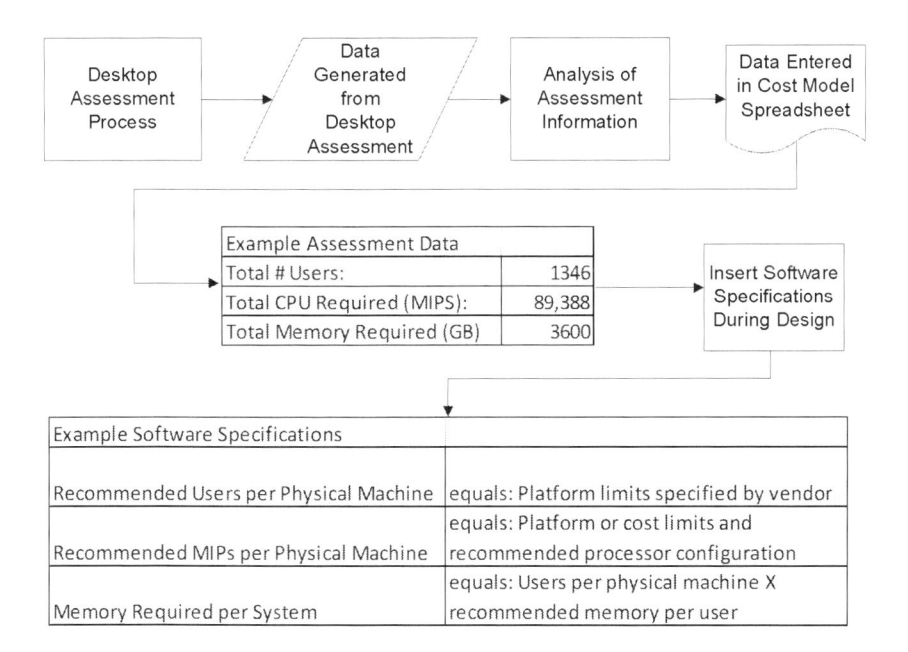

Example Software Specifications	
Recommended Users per Physical Machine	equals: Platform limits specified by vendor
Recommended MIPs per Physical Machine	equals: Platform or cost limits and recommended processor configuration
Memory Required per System	equals: Users per physical machine X recommended memory per user

Figure 4.4 — Assessment Data and Software Specifications

The second task the spreadsheet is used for is to attach the software solution and its required physical resources together inside of the cost model. This is the link between this section of the cost model and the centralized physical resources category discussed previously. You attach the two together by using the information from your assessment as source data to power the calculations for the software quantities outlined in your design. Once you have these calculations, you extract the hardware requirements and place them in the required physical resources category. You have now established a relationship from the virtual desktop platform to the centralized physical resources section of your design analysis. This process is outlined in Figure 4.5.

```
                                    Data
              Desktop             Generated         Analysis of       Data Entered
              Assessment            from           Assessment        in Cost Model
              Process              Desktop         Information        Spreadsheet
                                  Assessment
```

Example Assessment Data		
Total # Users:	1346	Insert Software
Total CPU Required (MIPS):	89,388	Specifications During Design
Total Memory Required (GB)	3600	

Example Software Specifications		
Recommended Users per Physical Machine	equals: Platform limits specified by vendor	Simple Formulas Populate Cost Model Spreadsheet with Hardware Requirements, Data Center Power Consumption, etc.
Recommended MIPs per Physical Machine	equals: Platform or cost limits and recommended processor configuration	
Memory Required per System	equals: Users per physical machine X recommended memory per user	

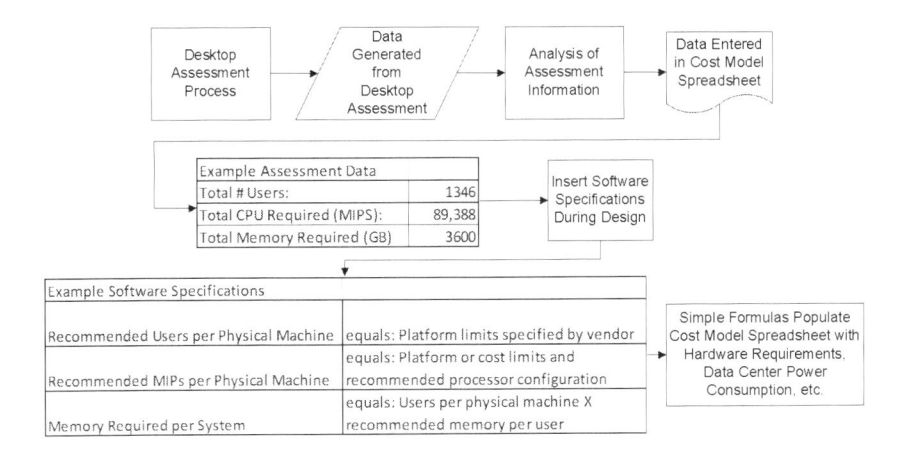

Figure 4.5 — How Simple Formulas from Virtual Desktop Platform Link to Hardware

With this link, there are a number of good comparisons you can perform to improve design. Examine how hardware changes will affect both the cost of centralized physical resources and the cost of software licenses.

- *What is the density of users per server?*
- *Can you double or triple this density for a small extra cost per server?*
- *Will the software support that kind of density on a single server?*
- *How is the software licensed?*

As you adjust the hardware to improve design, you will encounter a number of constraints, such as storage, memory and software maximums. Make note of the technical constraints and be wary of designs that get too close to them. Areas where a design recommendation competes with a constraint can result in risks that affect the success of a project. If you are comparing multiple software packages, compare the capabilities of different vendors and the cost differences of the hardware required to operate those solutions.

One important item to note is that there are a number of third-party solutions that perform enhanced user settings and "persona" management. These software packages go beyond the basic capabilities included in most virtual desktop platforms, giving you enhanced and centralized management of user data. They will often be a separate purchase, but because persona management can be a critical part of a virtual desktop solution, at least consider adding specific persona requirements to your requirements and design documents.

Within this section of the cost model spreadsheet, you will also need to add in any per-user licensing fees to cover the cost of these third party toolsets. There may also be additional costs under the administration section of your design analysis.

During virtual desktop platform selection, the administrative features of various software packages will be some of the most tangible and exciting benefits to your organization. These features, irrespective of cost and the platform's effect on centralized physical resources, may force all other considerations to be of secondary importance. If this is the case, how do you place a weight on the value of those administrative features? At some point, the benefits have to outweigh the cost burden, right? That is what the next section is all about — Administration!

Good starting points to begin the Virtual Desktop Platform portion of your design analysis:

1. Use your assessment information to determine the cost of software licenses you will need for a specific design.
2. Use these software quantities, together with vendor recommendations, to determine the amount of hardware that you need for a specific design.
3. Examine a solution's recommended hardware to make sure it maximizes user density, which can lower the total cost of required physical hardware or data center operating expenses.
4. Examine the way in which other technologies, such as application virtualization, can be used to lower these costs.

5. Be sure to pad the hardware and software constraints generated by the cost model so there is a margin for error.

6. In order to obtain an accurate forecast of solution cost, be sure to account for expected growth of the solution.

Administration

In the same way centralized physical resources need to be understood in terms of both the operating expense and the capital expense associated with different solutions, the administration of a virtual desktop platform needs to be understood in terms of your company's administrative starting and target states. Think back to the technology described to you in chapter two. When this sophisticated software and hardware is implemented, your company will require a change in the organizational structure of your desktop administrative staff and technology management processes.

Modeling this kind of organizational change is extremely difficult without knowing the full effects of a virtual desktop platform's administrative efficiencies or deficiencies. A vendor can set an expectation of management costs but, in the end, the numbers will vary for every company. Since this knowledge can only be gained through hindsight, cost estimations of the administrative change could be highly inaccurate.

Does this mean you shouldn't include this in your model? Absolutely not! Errors in this calculation provide you with a range of values. These cost values are important and come with the secondary understanding of the types of organizational change your company will undergo. Staffing and procedural changes will add weight to your selection of a virtual desktop platform and may "tip the scale" in favor of one solution over another.

If you think for a moment about the current state and composition of your organization's desktop administration capabilities, at the very highest level it is composed of *people*, *processes* and *technology*. The primary focus of this section of the model should be people and process. Technology has been addressed within the larger scope of this chapter, and there is only one technical calculation to include in this section of your cost model.

In any complex technology migration with a fundamental shift in platform or capability, there will be a technical element that cannot be migrated. The act of not migrating particular technical elements means that the cost of maintaining those systems will continue past the implementation of virtual desktops. For example, consider a hybrid virtual desktop deployment in which a company chooses to keep the operating system on the physical PC, but deploys virtual applications and user settings management. In this case, the software imaging system for the desktop operating systems will continue to be a cost.

The expense of licensing and using legacy technologies can be quite significant. If you know which technology you will not be able to migrate as part of a virtual desktop solution, ask *why*. Does it have something to do with the virtual desktop platform? Would choosing a different virtual desktop platform allow you to migrate this equipment and remove an additional support cost?

Like the other sections of this chapter, the content below simplifies a large body of knowledge to provide you with a starting point to understand the administration and support changes that will occur with a change to desktop virtualization. The following sections focus on cost impact and how to understand the various elements within the cost model spreadsheet. There is a secondary emphasis on the business process impact analysis that is part of the design analysis document set. This section is split into two parts. The first part addresses changes within the *support* area of desktop management, and the second addresses changes within *desktop administration*.

Administration — Support Staff

The vast majority of desktop organizations employ a system in which desktop support issues can be summarized and ranked by level 1, level 2 or level 3. Level 1 issues are the most basic problems, while level 3 is the most severe type of technical issue. Level 1 desktop issues are more typical than level 3, so it makes sense that many organizations require more level 1 staff than level 2 or level 3 staff. Any or all levels of support may also be outsourced to third parties and/or performed by different teams. Some separation usually exists between all levels of support resources.

The result is a system that resembles a pyramid, with a large base of level 1 staff, fewer level 2 staff, and even fewer level 3 staff. Staff could be separated by any number of items, such as schedules, culture, geography, management or salary. When considering payroll expense, level 1 staff are generally less qualified and less experienced, so their salaries are typically lower. Level 2 staff are paid at a mid-level salary, level 3 staff at the highest levels. What happens to support staff when you deploy virtual desktops? There are two parts to the answer; the first has to do with level 1 staff and the second with levels 2 and 3 staff.

Whether or not desktop support is outsourced, and all level 1 calls are handled in a call center run by an outside company in some other part of the world, level 1 staff will experience some degree of change. Imagine for a moment that you are dynamically creating a user's desktop upon their login to the network. The user has a simple thin client device, not a computer, and they are given a completely fresh desktop operating system, installed programs, user configuration, etc. — every time they login.

Remember back to chapter three where it was mentioned that understanding current support costs by software program and type was valuable. This is exactly where that kind of information can become important. Because the operating system is newly generated every time a user logs in, your company will see a decrease in support issues dealing with login or system errors. However, you will not see a significant decrease in other types of level 1 support issues, such as password resets, screen font sizes, and language, to name a few. With this configuration, the expected result would be fewer calls to the outsourced level 1 call center. If this is true, the level 1 staff headcount can be reduced.

In the area of level 1 application support, using application virtualization can lower the number of application errors that users experience. If you remember, chapter two discussed how these technologies separate the software from the user operating system and each other, making applications less prone to errors. The reduction in errors experienced by users will typically involve the operation of the application on the desktop, resulting in little to no change in internal application or user errors. For some of your company's most troublesome applications, this improvement could translate to a numerically significant reduction in support calls. If so, consider making the use of application virtualization a specific requirement and even detailing it within the cost model spreadsheet.

Fewer level 1 technical issues can also mean dramatic benefits for users. Once you have deployed your chosen virtual desktop solution, start comparing call levels and estimate the increases in user productivity. For the purposes of package selection and this section of your cost model, you should be able to estimate the reduction in level 1 support different virtual desktop solutions will offer by simply separating current issues into operating system and application-related level 1 errors. You can further refine these results by comparing them to information obtained from internal proof-of-concepts, proof-of-technologies, pilots, users, peers and vendor information.

The other half of the change in support involves level 2 and level 3 staff. Continuing with our example of a desktop that is generated automatically upon user login, what happens when a problem requires a phone call or support email? If the problem persists after basic troubleshooting, such as having the user log out and back in to the virtual desktop environment, the end user will need to be escalated past level 1 to level 2 (or 3). Put yourself in the mindset of the user at this point. He has tried logging in and there is a problem. He called level 1 support, which had him try a few easy troubleshooting steps in just a number of minutes. Because those did not work, the level 1 tech decides his call needs to be escalated.

Now, depending on the severity of the issue and maturity of your organization's technical support department, the typical desktop level 2 or 3 event will take anywhere between 1 to 8 hours to resolve. In our virtual desktop example, the employee is in a situation where he cannot work, making the technical support issue critical. If this is a centralized virtual desktop environment, the problem is probably not isolated and is affecting multiple users. This raises the profile of the support issue even further.

Two different actions should occur because of the escalation. The first task is mitigation, which involves simply moving users to backup resources to restore end user productivity. In this example, after mitigation, the users would be told to "try it again" and their logon to backup resources would be successful. Once the problem is mitigated, all necessary parties can be engaged to begin the repair, which is the second part of escalation.

This is an oversimplified example of the kinds of escalation scenarios that exist with virtual desktop solutions. The major point to consider is the centralized nature of virtual desktop problems. Except for client-side virtual desktops, most problems are going to be inside the data center or on the network, not at the user's client-access device. While this is good in that it reduces desk-side support visits, in order to avoid large productivity outages, your support staff will require the ability to rapidly escalate, mitigate and repair problems.

In order to accommodate this need, most companies will have to straighten their support personnel pyramid with more available level 2 and level 3 staff. Producing a thorough process impact analysis document will help provide an indication of the size of this potential change. Similar to the cost model changes, you can refine the process impact analysis by including information obtained from internal proof-of-concepts, pilots, the virtual desktop community, consultants and vendors.

In summary, the decreased need for level 1 support staff will be supplemented by an increase in level 2 and level 3 staff. As with any technology, properly engineered and managed solutions typically require few additional staff. Likewise, poorly implemented and managed solutions can result in dramatic business interruptions and put significant strain on desktop support capabilities (or in other words: fail to plan, plan to fail).

Administration - Management

The ability of a solution to be easily managed and deployed is an important consideration, leading to the last Administrative section to include in your documents. This last section is a top-level category covering system operation, maintenance and management. For large implementations, you will want to organize this into several different subgroups that are logically separated with the appropriate virtual desktop components.

For example, storage support may be part of the storage team's responsibilities, desktop applications part of the desktop team, data center resources part of the infrastructure team, and wide-area-network part of the network team. Smaller implementations will have overlaps in each of the individual areas and may have fewer subgroups. Each of these individual areas will need to be examined within the larger scope of your virtual desktop deployment. Remember that one of the values of the design analysis is being able to compare different virtual desktop solutions and to understand the impact of the technology on your organization.

In this section, you are examining the change in staff requirements required for operation and management of a virtual desktop solution. Once you break the solution into subgroups, you can estimate a range of percentage values for each of the different components. Together, these will represent the full-time headcount required to operate a particular set of virtual desktop technologies.

For some decision makers, estimating and considering staff changes may be extremely difficult, and could be perceived as unnecessary, overly complicated, or even impossible. The difficulty can stem from a number of constraints, such as lack of budget information and control, inability to forecast workflow, or an unwillingness to take leadership on the issue of staff change because it "is someone else's problem." If these real-world problems are insurmountable, make this a project risk and plan to resolve this issue during the proof-of-concept and pilot phases.

Let's go through an example to look at the level of change that is possible, and often necessary, with virtual desktops. Think back to the example used earlier in this section with the user that calls into the helpdesk because he cannot log in. The idea being presented was that an organization must be able to perform rapid escalation when basic troubleshooting steps do not work. Now, let's discuss this same incident, but in terms of helpdesk performance and reporting metrics.

In this example, a user is logging in and is unable to reach her virtual desktop. The helpdesk staff performs basic troubleshooting for 15 minutes, then realizes the problem is not isolated and it needs to be escalated. Upon escalation, the on-call staff takes 30 minutes to mitigate the problem so users are able to log in again. At this point, if you were to report on the cost of this issue, you could use a simple calculation like *total number of staff affected x mean salary x .75 hours*. If you want a more accurate calculation, you can begin to include additional items such as the cost of lost sales or the effect on production rate.

This example could be modified in a number of different ways to help illustrate this point. You could have had an automated alert that notified system operations of the problem, or maybe an automated nightly maintenance event failed and is causing the problem. No matter the cause of the event, the overall impact can be minimized with the right *people* and *processes*. Because of the new and enhanced processes that go along with virtual desktop management, you should begin planning for and understanding the effects of these changes through design, then fully experience and implement them during proof-of-concept and pilot.

Beginning to plan for these changes starts with your assessment and will continue into the design phase of your virtual desktop project. Begin by making assumptions of the staffing changes needed to meet production requirements, and then estimate the resulting financial and process impact. Consider outlining management functions in the requirements documents and then, within your cost model, you can calculate a range of values for resulting staffing changes, training expenses, etc. Refine these numbers based on the experience you have in proof-of-concept and pilot. As much as possible, make these calculations a function of your source assessment data.

> *Full understanding of the administration and support changes required for a virtual desktop implementation usually occurs during proof-of-concept and pilot activities. Central to these two activities are communication feedback loops. To increase your overall accuracy, consider the use of a 360-degree feedback loop in which you are collecting feedback from all levels of participants involved in the process, such as Virtual Desktop Administration, Helpdesk, Project Management, End Users, Managers and Stakeholders.*

Good starting points for you to begin the Administration portion of your design analysis:

1. Know what legacy technology you are going to leave in your organization and its annual cost of maintenance.
2. Extract per-application and per-issue support information from your helpdesk ticketing system. Classify areas where this information will change as a result of virtual desktop implementations.
3. Analyze the maturity of levels 1, 2 and 3 staff and their ability to work with virtual desktop technologies.

Applications

While administration has numerous variables that will involve some assumption and estimation, *applications* are the exact opposite. Applications are quite simple really — they exist and they need to be used by end users. During the virtual desktop assessment process you will generate two lists: one of installed applications and another of used applications. You could also expand this list to add or categorize other applications by employee role, department, position, or many other types of criteria.

What may (or may not) surprise you about these lists is the quantity and variation of applications. Many moderately-sized organizations have hundreds, or even thousands, of applications. Take an enterprise with 10,000 users and 800 applications. How do you determine the influence of 800 different applications on a virtual desktop design, much less the *cost* of the impact on design?

This is kind of like a chicken and egg problem (you know, which one came first and all that). You could approach this problem in several ways:

1. You decide on your virtual desktop platform and figure out the best way to deliver applications through this platform to end users.

2. You categorize and examine the applications and figure out the most efficient and cost-effective way to deliver applications to end users. This might be part of an application compatibility and rationalization effort when considering a migration to Windows 7.

3. You don't really change much and deliver applications the same way you are now.

The truth is that you will likely do some variation on all three of these. For the purposes of your cost model, before designing a solution, all you need to do is categorize applications into those that you will change and those that you won't. Focus on the keyword *deliver* in the three approaches outlined above.

Of the 800 applications in the example company, let's see what happens when they are categorized into those that need to change and those that don't. Assume approximately 150 of those applications are web applications. Of these 150 web applications, 125 of them work with any web browser and do not require any special consideration, while 25 require a mix of specific browser versions and add-ons. Because 125 of the applications will work, you can use the third approach from the above list and deliver them in the same way you are doing now, with no impact on the overall virtual desktop design.

Even though they don't have an effect on application virtualization, whenever working with an application inventory, it is best to be thorough and still list these apps in the cost model as a category. At this point, the analysis of the applications would look something like this:

125	Approach 3 - Compatible Web Applications
25	Web Applications w/ Special Requirements
675	Unknown Applications

| 800 | Total Applications |

Let's forget about the "Web Applications with Special Requirements" category right now and move on to the rest of the unknown applications. These are going to fit into two other categories and include either applications executed on the virtual desktops, or applications delivered to users using session virtualization. If you remember back to chapter two, session virtualization is a technology in which the application is run on a server in the data center with only visual information sent to the end user. As an application, it looks, acts and behaves just like a locally-installed application and can be run at a user endpoint or inside of a virtual desktop.

Applications using session virtualization do not need to be changed for a virtual desktop implementation, so they will have no impact on design and overall solution cost — just like the compatible web applications. If 75 of the applications in our example company are run this way, our analysis of the applications looks something like this:

125	Approach 3 - Compatible Web Applications
25	Web Applications w/ Special Requirements
75	Approach 3 - Session Virtualization
600	Locally Executed Applications

800	Total Applications

Of the 800 total applications, only 625 need to be considered as part of the virtual desktop design, with 600 of those being locally-executed applications and 25 as web applications with special requirements. Notice the words *locally executed* are used to describe these applications. In order to understand how to handle these applications, remember back to chapter two, where the concept of *Application Virtualization* was discussed. Virtual applications were described as gifts or packages you give to someone. To use what is inside, all the person has to do is open the package. Virtual applications are independent packages that can be placed on a virtual desktop and executed—no installation necessary.

You need to consider two different approaches to understand how the remaining 625 applications will affect your virtual desktop design and cost model. The desired method is to turn these applications into virtual application packages. The less desirable approach is to install these applications inside of the virtual desktops. Why is one approach preferred over the other? Simply stated, application virtualization lowers application support costs and isolates applications so they are more compatible and easier to distribute, maintain and setup than their installed counterparts.

Your default approach should be to use application virtualization wherever possible. Install applications inside a virtual desktop only as a last resort, or in cases where the use of installed applications will not dramatically affect your virtual desktop design or maintenance expense. A good example might be when you have lots of virtual desktops with only a few pieces of software installed. In a case like this, there might not be any benefit to having the applications packaged.

Take note of the 25 web applications that are bundled and require special browsers and add-ons. Why is this? You can create special Internet browser virtual application packages for all of the different browsers and plug-ins that need to be supported. This is true even if two or more of the web applications use add-ons that are incompatible. Because application virtualization isolates applications from one another, you can run incompatible software packages together on the same virtual or physical desktop. Application virtualization provides a solution for dealing with troublesome or outdated web applications that are incompatible with the most recent Internet browsers.

After grouping all of your applications into these high-level categories, you still need to determine their effect on your virtual desktop design and cost model. One great aspect of application virtualization is that it can exist independently of your virtual desktop platform, or it can be tightly integrated with the platform, or both. In all of these cases, two costs need to be considered: *application packaging* and *platform/licensing*.

Application Packaging

Application packaging is the process of turning an application into a virtual application. Called "packaging," experts typically claim that it is half art and half science. Whatever the case, packaging takes between three and twenty-plus hours per application. Packaging involves creation of the virtual package, testing by technical staff and then acceptance testing by end users. These tasks can be taken care of in-house by your staff or outsourced to a third party specializing in this type of work. For large-batch operations, such as the 600 applications in our example, it is typically more cost-effective to outsource this work and develop in-house expertise for maintenance, updates and occasional "one-off" packaging needs.

For complex packaged applications with lots of parts and tight integration with the operating system, consider adding specific application use cases in both the business and technical portions of your document set. Understanding the behavior and use of a complex application from the user's perspective, coupled with technical information on how the application behaves, can be a useful tool for application packagers and can also assist in checking the quality of the resulting packaged applications. Within the cost model, each application or application group will have a cost associated with packaging, testing and licensing.

Software Licensing

The licensing cost might be included as a feature of your virtual desktop platform, or as a separate software product. There is also the possibility of different license types for different features. Choosing a virtual application platform that is part of a larger virtual desktop suite might allow you to have a higher amount of compatibility and functionality, along with easier maintenance, management or distribution. Choosing virtual application software outside of the virtual desktop suite could reduce licensing costs or provide you with advantages in packaging, performance or distribution.

Once applications are grouped, and you have determined the list of applications you want to virtualize, the final cost and overall effect on your cost model is comprised of the cost to *package* your applications and the cost to *license* the virtual application software. If you have troublesome applications with high support costs, you may choose to estimate cost savings for these applications in the areas of installation or maintenance. These calculations can be done nearly independently of all other sections of the cost model and, as mentioned previously, many organizations choose to virtualize applications as a first step towards desktop virtualization.

Good starting points for you to begin the Applications portion of your design analysis:

1. Make sure you have an accurate application inventory, including lists of both *installed* and *used* applications.

2. Categorize applications by delivery method, paying particular attention to those that will affect your design analysis.

3. Consider special application use cases for complex and highly integrated applications to aid in packaging and checking quality.

4. Review third-party application packaging services to understand per-application packaging costs.

Client Access

The literal "end" of virtual desktop technologies is the users, and the technology that allows them to experience and use applications. Remember, the user should be placed on a pedestal and your virtual desktop solution should enable users to have a great experience and be at least as productive as they are right now. Equal performance is often subjective and can therefore be very elusive and hard to determine. You will never make *every* user happy, so "equal performance" will vary in meaning from an "it works every time" kind of reliability to faster application startup to faster printing to any combination of the factors that make up the client computing experience.

Since users have so many factors they use to determine performance, how do you begin to consider the *Client Access* category before you have a design or have performed a proof-of-concept? Let's look at the information you get from an assessment and the design analysis.

As discussed in chapter three, the virtual desktop assessment will give you a lot of information about your end user's computing environment. These valuable statistics tell you about the user's experience in quantifiable measurements, such as how long it takes to start an application, the number of hours specific types of users use their PCs, and overall performance of the PCs while they are being used. This information is all extremely important and, with one exception, it is almost completely irrelevant to the Client Access category. What?! How can that be?

That exception will be covered in a moment, but let's first address why this information is irrelevant to the Client Access category. If you think about what the assessment information is used for, it is typically to ensure the devices providing the user with their virtual desktop perform at the same level as their current physical desktop. In the case of your design analysis and actual solution design, these elements are covered in the *Physical Resources* and *Virtual Desktop Platform* sections. This means the Client Access category of your design analysis needs to cover only the physical device and network connection used to service a virtual desktop.

The exception to this broad generalization has to do with client-side virtual desktops. If you are considering this technology for certain user groups, you will need to use the assessment information to ensure the new client-access devices perform as well (or better) than the physical PCs they are replacing. In your cost model, consider simplifying the assessment results with categories of users that have low-performance, medium-performance and high-performance needs. Once you know how many of each type of user you have, it is easy to calculate the impact on your solution's cost.

For a centralized virtual desktop deployment, the performance characteristics of a user's computing experience are accounted for in the *Physical Resources* and *Virtual Desktop Platform* sections of your design analysis. This leaves only two considerations to include within your analysis documents and cost model. These are the *network connections* used to service the virtual desktop user and the *physical devices* used for client access.

Network Connections

You should involve network engineers and desktop virtualization experts in the evaluation and recommendations of changes that need to be made to the network servicing end users from a central location.

These changes should guarantee good performance of virtual desktops and may need to be stipulated within the requirements documents. Within your cost model, you will want to list any equipment expenses and the monthly increase or decrease in cost for the network connections needed to service users from the data center hosting the desktops.

When considering the changes in network connections for virtual desktops, examine the protocol used to connect a user to their virtual desktop. There are many competing protocols which will work with various virtual desktop platforms and each has its own strengths and weaknesses. Your choice of a virtual desktop platform could be driven in part by certain network connection requirements. A simple example is a requirement that states, "Virtual desktops must perform within well defined, acceptable levels over the Internet." Your design may address this requirement by proposing the use of a certain virtual desktop platform that uses a protocol designed specifically for this purpose, and that protocol may in turn require specific network conditions that increase or decrease the costs listed in your cost model.

Understanding network changes can be one of the most difficult aspects of this process. Networks are kind of like opinions—every person has one, they are all different, and not all of them are logical. Because of this, consider breaking up network connectivity into a few different categories in your model and documents. Within the cost model, there will be the physical devices and monthly connection fees to account for. The requirements document should include the different networks with which the solution must work. Requirements can be stated directly, such as, "The virtual desktops provided to offshore workers must work using existing network connections." When these requirements are outlined, the design document can then account for the configurations necessary to meet these requirements.

Client-Access Devices

Once you have considered the type of network connection needed to service a virtual desktop, the very last element is the client-access device. A number of technologies can be used for this purpose and were highlighted in chapter two. Focus first on articulating the requirements of device endpoints, being sure to choose the right device for your users and administration staff. Once the requirements are outlined and incorporated into the design, choosing a device should be relatively easy.

Client-access devices used to access a virtual desktop vary from a full PC to a low-power "smart" PC to minimalist thin clients, smartphones and tablets. A number of elements should be compared when analyzing the cost of the devices, such as the expected lifespan and maintenance costs of the thin client devices versus PCs. The refresh cycle for thin clients can be quite long, and they can often be fully maintained from a centralized management system that the vendor provides, minimizing the need for onsite visits. You may choose to put the support savings in the *Administration* portion of your cost model, or attach it to the physical device that is used.

Another significant item to model is the power consumption of the client-access devices. The *Physical Resources* category outlined the fact that, while you are adding power consumption inside the data center, this can be offset by the reduction in power of the client-access devices. Client-side power savings often is part of a different budget, so there may not be an ability to realize the savings within the IT department's budget. For full PCs, an easy way to make this calculation is to figure 150W power consumption for each PC and use the assessment information for number of hours in use to understand the total KWh consumed by PCs. This assumes that a PC goes to sleep when it is not in use.

Beyond the cost of the physical devices needed, software licensing is possibly a separate category. This is especially true if you are using full PCs or re-using computers because these configurations have a lot of software licensing requirements. There are some very good open-source (read "free") software packages based on Linux distributions that can be used to turn a computer into a thin-client-like device with the only cost being the time it takes to configure the solution. The major drawback with this approach is limited support for certain configurations, so open-source clients might only meet a subset of your requirements.

Good starting points for you to begin the Client Access portion of your design analysis:

1. Put together a team of desktop virtualization and network engineering staff to outline the network requirements that will affect client access.
2. List general requirements for your client-access devices and put cost estimates into your cost model.
3. Consider power savings at the client-access level versus the increase that may be seen inside of the data center. Consider how to apply this savings to the right budget.

Summary: Assessment Analysis → Design → Design Analysis

This chapter was written with the idea that after completing an assessment you will begin to set requirements, perform design and understand costs. Once you have chosen a solution design that meets your requirements, you can go back to the analysis and understand the relationships between the five major areas of a virtual desktop system. There is significant value in understanding these relationships, as minor details can cause changes in the overall solution costing six figures or more.

The ability to estimate the level of effort for implementation using the cost model was intentionally left out of this chapter. While not an impossible calculation, so many unquantifiable variables exist that the results of such a calculation description in this book will be largely inaccurate. Level of effort should be determined during the different project planning phases, incorporate vendor and consultant estimates and recommendations, and also take into account the knowledge and maturity gained during proof-of-concept tasks. Proof-of-concept goals that incorporate learning and mock-execution of processes can be highly valuable to assist in quantifying the time required to perform certain tasks.

This chapter has hopefully provided the guidance to help you produce a detailed document set that will:

1. Help you understand what a specific design will **truly** cost.

2. Create firm requirements that will improve a design to **meet company needs.**

With this information, you can compare different solution designs and possibly continue use and refinement of the cost model through the proof-of-concept, pilot, production and maintenance phases of your implementation. When used this way, the model can become a resource to aid in forecasting and providing quantifiable, detailed information about your solution.

Chapter 5:
Let's Talk Virtual Desktops

In an ideal world, companies would use technology to solve problems in the most efficient and cost-effective manner possible. Orders not shipping fast enough? A straightforward solution might be to implement three different technologies proven to increase shipping speed by 40% or more.

For every project, there would be a well-written and easily communicated statement of the problem and the technologies needed to create the solution. In addition, the technologies outlined in that statement would align with the problem, rather than being "made to fit."

But, this is the real world. It is a place where people, government, competition, leadership, relationships, innovation and the market all combine to create both the problems and the solutions that solve them. Do company policies, government regulation, leadership personalities and vendor relationships play a significant part in the way your company solves problems? You bet they do.

The preceding chapters have hopefully given you a basic idea of how to begin thinking about virtual desktop technologies to address the problems you are trying to solve. If you are in the proof-of-concept or pilot phases, you should already be well on your way to addressing your first set of problems and considering how to approach additional, more complex scenarios. In either case, real-world constraints will influence your decisions about the best solutions for your company.

For example, a past leader's decision might leave you stuck using a less-desirable technology as your virtual desktop platform. When trying to correct problems, you might encounter technical groups that are insensitive to your needs. Or, it could be that management simply lacks the desire or ability to assist the project in the necessary way.

Each company will have different motivations driving a desktop virtualization project. Some want the innovation or improvements created by the technology, like more efficiency in administration and faster desktop provisioning. For others, the drivers are the result of change, like new regulations, mergers, security changes, outsourcing, OS migrations or PC aging. Regardless of the project driver, real-world constraints and the desire for a successful implementation mean it is absolutely essential that all parties involved in implementation and decision making communicate about virtual desktop technology.

Communicating about virtual desktops can be a unique challenge. First of all, we *are* talking about desktops, which have mainly been in the form of PCs since the days of DOS. While they have changed a lot, they really haven't. Each user has one, each one has an OS, each OS has software installed, each can get a virus—you get the idea. Understanding the change virtual desktops represent could be quite difficult and some people will need to see an actual demonstration of the technology. People literally have to "touch" it, ask questions and discuss it for a while before starting to understand.

Second, virtual desktop projects involve different levels of staff, many of whom will not have intimate knowledge of the desktop. Even some of the most hardcore tech-heads will not understand or appreciate the reasons for some aspects of virtual desktop design or implementation. Sometimes the technical staff, because they know servers, believes they also know desktops running in the data center. Additionally, decision makers may not appreciate the risks or subtleties and might put together arbitrary timelines or have unrealistic expectations. If that's not enough, some folks just won't believe in virtual desktops at all!

Finally, virtual desktops have numerous value propositions. Some of these will align with project requirements and others will fall into the "nice to have, but not really necessary to meet project objectives" area. Other technical solutions often present this same situation, but there is an important differentiator between virtual desktops and other technology that needs to be recognized in order to communicate effectively.

For a good comparison, think about a luxury automobile. A luxury car has the basic features you use every day and certainly expect — the starter, the engine, speedometer, and doors. The enhanced features border on "have-to-have" and "nice-to-have" and include things like power windows and mirrors, automatic locks, air conditioning, defrost, and fold-down rear seats. There are also the regulatory features like bumpers, air bags and exhaust systems you pay for. At the high end of the feature list are the luxury items like GPS systems, memory seats and automatic parallel parking.

A technical implementation typically involves a subset of features from within all of these categories — basic, enhanced, regulatory and luxury. For a software implementation, you might need eight components of the server operating system. For a data migration, you might need specific features from a variety of tools. For a network upgrade, you might need specific devices with specific ports to run a few different communications protocols. Within these examples, and most technical projects in general, there is an impact to the organization. This impact includes both the parties involved in a project and the effects of the project's end state.

Compare the projects above to one with a larger impact, such as a companywide ERP implementation. Companywide projects might touch every business unit, and a majority of business processes, through an implementation lasting several years. Even if a project is implemented in small phases and starts with a limited scope, some high-level planning is still required to comprehend the total size of the impact. Even a small virtual desktop implementation deserves discussion and analysis with numerous executives, IT staff and vendors.

Starting the Virtual Desktop Conversation

The first conversations about virtual desktops often begin as a result of educational marketing by outside vendors, who will present case studies, research findings, or value propositions to prospective decision makers throughout the company. While this content likely has elements of truth, it is *designed to be compelling and provoke an action and response from the audience.* More often than not, *it is not vendor neutral*, nor will it contain comprehensive and focused information for the specific needs of the audience.

When virtual desktops evolve beyond an interest in educational marketing materials or water cooler talk, it's time for deeper conversations focusing on the impacts of the technology within each department or the entire company. If you are at this stage, consider how to capture the needs of your company in a formal Request for Proposal (RFP) or Request for Quotation (RFQ).

The point of early conversations, presentations, and planning sessions should be to *provide a foundation with which to successfully start a virtual desktop project*. The involvement of different staff and vendors will be relative to the project timeline. For example, you might not need to involve all business unit leaders in early discussions about virtual desktops, but you should at least involve representatives of those parties impacted by the project.

These early discussions are not only to address overall project drivers and value propositions. Project leaders should be involved in communication about all of the possible impacts and implications different consumers of the technology consider important.

On the technical side, discussions should ensue with the CIO and managers of data centers, security, networks, virtualization and desktops, to name a few. On the business side, strategy should be discussed with *at least* executive leadership and affected business unit leaders. It is best if proof-of-concept and pilot representatives are also included early in the project.

These discussions could be educational and/or solution-oriented, and used to set expectations, or specifically designed to get buy-in from meeting participants. Since virtual desktops will impact all areas of the company, including each user's personal computing experience, the value perceived by one party will be different than that perceived by another.

A typical meeting about virtual desktops might have one party focused on security and management, while another is focused on reliability and end user experience. Given that these technologies have such a broad reach, it is critical that project leaders effectively summarize and communicate virtual desktop information, and that all concerns be understood, addressed and expressed appropriately in the project's working documents.

The result of these early meetings could add to the list of project drivers and/or requirements, and thus add to the complexity of your project. Beyond using the natural charm and wit most project leaders are born with, information from vendors, seminars, case studies and material presented in previous chapters of this book can assist in early communications. Project leaders should consider keeping early communication at a higher-level to improve overall understanding about the desirable project qualities, business cases, project vision and impact of virtual desktop solutions. The following pages provide examples of high-level summaries of value propositions.

Virtual Desktop Value Propositions

The simplest view of the desktop computing experience might be as follows: every day, at any company, computers are logged into in the morning, logged out of in the evening, and in between, people are working. In the real world, layers upon layers of subtlety are added to this process. Things happen at login; applications from around the globe are accessed; information is backed up; mistakes are made; users get frustrated; computers break; software has to be updated; employees are hired and terminated; staff need to work remotely; and offices are opening or closing.

It can be beneficial if early communication around virtual desktops does not revolve around the *effect* the technology has on the individual process layers, but instead on the *strategic value* of these tools to support the goals of the entire company. The following sections offer some examples of common company strategies—business continuity, outsourcing, security, and productivity—to demonstrate high-level communication of value propositions and business strategy.

Example #1: Business Continuity

With any sort of technical project, a topic that is often (and should always be) considered is business continuity planning (BCP), which is all of the activities that an organization performs to ensure the organization's services are consistently made available and recoverable. Because BCP includes far more than just technical matters, disaster recovery is considered a subset of business continuity and should therefore be addressed within the scope of an organization's entire BCP processes.

With the physical desktops in your company, what happens when a disaster occurs and employees need access to applications and information to continue operations? Do the technical portions of your business continuity plan give you the ability to deploy 300 new desktops to an alternate site to restore productivity? Are employees only able to access critical information from home or a small emergency site?

Virtual desktops enable new capabilities within business continuity planning. An easy way to think about and categorize these capabilities is to imagine two BCP domains, one that contains everything inside of the data center, and another that includes everything outside of the data center.

For a centralized deployment in the data center, the virtual desktops are all running on servers and storage that should be very similar, if not identical, to all the other systems in that same location. Since those systems can be replicated to a second location, recovery of virtual desktops might not be a significant challenge. In fact, with the right set of requirements and the right solution design, in theory you should be able to enable recovery of the virtual desktops by using modified versions of your existing technologies and processes.

Outside of the data center, the primary concern will be how employees access their information. Under normal operations, access would be through a workstation, laptop or thin client type device remotely or from within the office. In the event business continuity plans are in effect, users just need devices that can access the Internet and operate the virtual desktops. These devices could be at a secondary site or at home.

Imagine a BCP scenario in which there is a massive snow storm and some offices need to be temporarily closed. Now, imagine a more complex BCP scenario in which a storm or natural disaster creates a total power outage. In either case, as long as users have access to a PC and the Internet, they can access some or all of their applications through a secure website.

Value proposition:

Virtual desktops have the ability to improve business continuity and disaster recovery.

Example #2: Outsourcing

Whether we like it or not, today's global economy has forced many companies to outsource some aspect of their operations. Imagine being able to provide any application, to any location, *without* any special equipment or staff, *with* all the security and resources you use to service existing users and without data ever leaving the data center. This is one of the killer applications of virtual desktop technology. A few technical limitations exist, but they can be overcome with proper design, centralized placement and good network connections.

This kind of flexibility is an exciting benefit for executives, and even entire organizations, seeking to advance outsourcing initiatives. With centralized virtual desktops comes the ability to access any kind of sophisticated application set with only the most basic infrastructure.

Several kinds of outsourcing relationships are available and it is important that you first understand the types your company has in place, then choose a virtual desktop solution to address your specific needs. This does not mean you will have specialized solutions for the different relationships, but the virtual desktop platform you choose should include design variations and subsets of features that will meet those needs. Being able to securely serve multiple relationships should be listed as a requirement and considered a significant aspect of design.

Outsourced virtual desktops deal with extreme distances and time-zone differences. Do not underestimate the effects and implications of these variables. If virtual desktop administrators are in Canada, and the outsourced relationships are in South Asia, there are some real barriers to successfully implementing virtual desktops. To keep the system operational, some staff might need to work different shifts than they currently do, or staff could require more advanced monitoring abilities or intimate support of network engineers and external vendors. For many companies, these needs require change that can only be accomplished with the understanding and support of the organization's leaders.

Value proposition:

With a few changes to IT operations, virtual desktops can enhance and enable all kinds of outsourcing relationships.

Example #3: Security

The technical aspects of security for virtual desktops are out of the scope and page count of this book, but virtual desktops have enormous security implications for the desktop. An easy way to outline security is generally within two domains—one being the technology experts who specialize in the field, and the other being the configurations required by company and regulatory standards. Near the beginning of a project, company and regulatory standards will be some of the most frequent topics of conversation.

Central to many of these conversations will be the topic of where information is stored and how information is accessed. For example, with virtual desktops, it is entirely plausible to have a solution in which information cannot be stored at the user's end point. No USB Sticks, local C drives or copy/paste to external sources. This level of control allows you to send desktops to new places, such as out to unsecure geographies or in to highly secured locations.

All vendors have numerous examples of virtual desktop platforms and connection brokers to demonstrate the various ways to securely access a virtual desktop. Those examples could be extremely useful in demonstrating where your proposed solutions fit within company security requirements.

Another popular topic of conversation is the additional levels of security available with the advanced management capabilities of virtual desktop platforms. Typical deployments include new operating system functions, such as the option to refresh the desktop back to the standard secure image after a user logs out, erasing any changes the user or malware made. Often you can apply security patches globally across virtual desktops with only a few mouse clicks.

Furthermore, you can even introduce significantly isolated application and data layers, as well as strict enforcement of which software users are allowed to operate. All of these functions are possible to some degree with physical desktops, but virtual desktops make them more manageable, flexible and secure.

Value proposition:

Virtual desktops offer significant improvements to security, specifically by enabling more secure access to, and management of, the desktop, applications and user data.

Example #4: Employee Productivity

Conversations about employee productivity depend largely on the current state of your company's desktop environment. If you are in an organization with a successful desktop environment, your users already have a reliable desktop experience. In this case, the topics being discussed will center around enhanced capabilities and more flexibility. If you are in an environment where the desktop is despised by the users, the focus of conversation will primarily center around increased reliability, with all other aspects addressed as secondary concerns.

As with any technical solution, reliability also brings a lot of "IF" baggage with it.

- *IF the system is designed well, you can have a virtual desktop solution that is extremely reliable.*
- *IF the system is managed well, there will be few, if any, outages related to administrative mistakes.*
- *IF the helpdesk is trained and staffed properly, users will have minimal frustration with their lack of physical control.*

Yes, several paragraphs could be filled with "IF" statements, but since you have read the preceding chapters, you get the point. **Reliability should be the end result of any and all aspects of a virtual desktop system.**

Since this is the case, reliability should be a major point in all conversations with leadership, and the first or second requirement you outline. Once that is addressed, a number of calculations can be performed to understand and communicate what enhanced productivity means for your company.

When you present the positive effects of virtual desktops such as enhanced remote capabilities, reduced support incidents, better reliability and improved isolation, use data you have in your own company to support your calculations. For example, how much is a day of productivity worth for an office that is closed several times a year due to inclement weather? How much is it worth to keep a superstar employee that is relocating and otherwise would be forced to quit her job?

Restoring lost productivity, and retaining valuable employees, are intangibles that are difficult to calculate, but still very relevant. These intangibles, and even overall reliability itself, should be looked at as the macro aspects of virtual desktops.

The desktop computing experience also has many micro components, such as the length of time it takes for the start menu to appear after a user clicks on it, or how long it takes for a program to start or perform a function. While these might seem insignificant individually, delays and problems with the normal user-interface components of the virtual desktop can quickly add up and counter any macro gains that you might achieve.

Monitoring and reporting capabilities need to be in place to ensure this situation does not occur. In addition, proper planning is essential if the system will ever be scaled out to accommodate additional users and/or new pieces of software. Scaling out or updating an application can have a negative impact on the user interface and overall performance of virtual desktops and employee productivity.

Value proposition:

With a reliable virtual desktop system, there can be quantifiable gains in employee productivity.

Why Communication = Success

Communication is essential. This cannot be stressed enough. Any project impacting a significant portion of a company, at any point, needs to involve communication to and between all of the affected parties. By their very nature, virtual desktops represent an enormous risk for a company if not implemented and managed correctly. Preceding chapters have discussed respecting users, using the right technologies, assessing the existing environment, and coming up with a proper design analysis. None of these things matter if project leaders do not communicate with the right people at the right times.

Speak to affected parties as early as possible in the project, even if only to make introductions, set expectations, answer questions and build trust. Throughout the implementation process, project leaders will be involved in feedback loops with all levels of technical, managerial and end user hierarchies. Speaking *with*, rather than *to*, affected parties will result in a more successful and collaborative virtual desktop implementation. Virtual desktop project leaders need to consider outside parties as subject matter experts and value their input and recommendations appropriately.

As mentioned earlier, increased communication can lead to an increase in requirements. For large organizations, this could challenge project leadership with the sheer complexity or size of the task. Disciplined project scoping can solve this problem. By listing features and wish list items in a comprehensive manner, and performing a cost benefit analysis, you can determine the must-have features. Organize that list into phases, involving stakeholders throughout this project planning process.

Proper communication leads to a reduction in risk, a thorough design, a properly scoped project, an understanding of value, accurate expectations, and the support and trust of the stakeholders. If you still doubt the value of abundant and worthwhile communication and involvement, just answer this question:

"Would you rather implement virtual desktops having a thorough design with an audience that trusts and appreciates the values of the solution?" Of course you would!

Conclusion:
Let the Games Begin

What an exciting time for the desktop! It is being recreated and transformed at an astounding pace. The virtual desktop is one piece of that change—a new state of the desktop made up of many different technologies. While there is no doubt a 'tipping point' has been reached in the evolution of the desktop, in some ways we are in the earliest stages of this adventure. Big announcements are being made all the time about new and improved products. Some of the newest virtual desktop developments will have enormous implications for the future of this technology, as well as the future of the people and companies using it.

For the people who use virtual desktops to do their work, a good end-state after implementation is one in which the users barely even notice a change. In reality, this means their operating system, applications and user data all work together with functionality equal to that of a normal physical desktop. The perfect end-state involves alignment of the design and value propositions of the virtual desktop with the user's use case. Users should be able to do things they were not able to do before. They should enjoy a *better* desktop; one that allows them to compute easier with real gains in their productivity.

The high-level technical categories outlined in chapter two have layers of subtlety not discussed in this book. Each of the various technical categories is filled by numerous companies selling products or services to address the needs of the market. Some of these products have plenty of features that allow their use in nearly every imaginable user use case. Technical staff may take hundreds of hours to become proficient in their use. It may take thousands of hours to properly implement these solutions inside your company. Given that hurdle, other "point products" in the market are designed to solve specific needs in a simple and straightforward manner. If implementation of an entire suite of technical products seems overly complex for your company, consider some of these simpler solutions or techniques.

Every decision made about these technologies must include an understanding of the direct consequences of that decision to the business, the users and the administrators. The end user sits at the apex of the virtual desktop. While there are all kinds of value propositions and reasons to virtualize the desktop, you cannot forget that *people* are the consumers served by this technology. It is important that everyone involved in a virtual desktop project knows successful adoption by the user community is absolutely crucial to the project's success. The need for a *quantifiably* productive user experience should be on par with other top project goals.

As you begin to travel the road toward desktop virtualization, consider using success criteria to define completion of the project. These criteria will be generated and expanded during different project stages. Prior to the assessment phase, the success criteria will be broad statements that lack strict definition. After assessment, there will be an expanded set of success criteria that are more accurate. The design analysis phase will document a solution and prepare an organization for entering the proof-of-concept phase.

Throughout the proof-of-concept portions of a virtual desktop project, the knowledge you gain may result in conditions being set upon the success criteria. Once the proof-of-concept has been completed, the system is ready to be piloted with *real* users.

The pilot phase is typically a set of iterative expansions, starting with a few technical champions and expanding in larger and larger increments. The pilot phase should not end on a timeline, but instead when all of the project success criteria have been met. The end of a pilot involves a transition plan that expands use of the designed system to the entire scope of users. You transition into production from the pilot phase.

The quality of a virtual desktop project is going to depend on the quality of work during the assessment and design phases. Organizations must perform an assessment of the current desktop environment to quantify the most critical information about a company's users, applications, data and physical PCs. This information, combined with key information from support staff and subject-matter-experts, can then be fully analyzed. The analysis of the assessment information will help reduce the total number of project assumptions and overall project risk.

Assessment analysis naturally leads to formal project requirements. Once project requirements are outlined, the assessment information is used to help with the solution design. The process of design analysis allows decision makers to understand the relationships that exist between project requirements and a solution for implementation. Examination of these relationships further reduces project assumptions and risk, and simultaneously improves the virtual desktop design.

A strong virtual desktop design ensures the proof-of-concept is not a wasted effort. The purpose of a proof-of-concept is to demonstrate a technology can, in reality, solve a set of business problems. This requires the business problems to be stated as accurately as possible. Proof-of-concepts that demonstrate basic virtual desktop functionality are only valuable if that is what is defined within the project success criteria, and thus representative of what the end user will truly be using. If there are doubts as to whether your organization is ready to run a proof-of-concept, consider adding a proof-of-technology step between design and proof-of-concept. This will validate and prove the use of a technology in a specific way.

Communicating with all parties involved is critical throughout all project stages. Besides technical staff, include representatives of all teams involved in the project. Consider how to educate and explain how a transition to virtual desktops will affect business processes and employees. Involve and inform people early on in the project. Plan to communicate extensively with end users during the latter stages of a virtual desktop implementation. Have a detailed communication plan and use thorough, 360-degree feedback loops during the proof-of-concept and pilot phases.

Note from the author...

And with that, you have reached the end of this book and the beginning of your game-changing adventure. I truly hope you have enjoyed learning about the exciting world of virtual desktops as much as I have enjoyed writing about it. Please contact me personally with any comments or questions. You can find my contact information on this book's website, www.demystifyingthevirtualdesktop.com. I wish you much success in your future virtual desktop endeavors.

- Michael

Made in the USA
Charleston, SC
07 July 2013